THE Quilt Patch

FAIRFAX VIRGINIA

LESLIE ANNE PFEIFER

That Patchwork Place®

Credits
Editor-in-Chief . . . . Barbara Weiland
Technical Editor . . . . Janet White
Managing Editor . . . . Greg Sharp
Copy Editor . . . . Tina Cook
Proofreader . . . . Leslie Phillips
Design Director . . . . Judy Petry
Cover and Text Designer . . . . . David Chrisman
Production Assistant . . . . Shean Bemis
Technical Illustrator . . . . .Laurel Strand
Illustration Assistant . . . . Lisa McKenney
Decorative Art . . . . .Laurie Jensen
Photographer . . . . Brent Kane

The Quilt Patch

© 1995 by Leslie Anne Pfeifer
That Patchwork Place, Inc.
PO Box 118, Bothell, WA 98041-0118 USA

Printed in Hong Kong
00 99 98 97 96 95   6 5 4 3 2 1

Library of Congress Cataloging-in-Publication Data
Pfeifer, Leslie Anne,
   The quilt patch / Leslie Anne Pfeifer.
      p. cm. — (New American quilt shop series)
   ISBN 1-56477-110-5
   1. Patchwork—Patterns. 2. Patchwork quilts. 3. Quilt Patch
(Fairfax, Va.) I. Title   II. Series.
   TT835. P4495 1995
   746.46—dc20   95-18282
                                CIP

Dedication

A wise person once said that if we have just one true
friend in our lives, we can count ourselves among the
very lucky. I am fortunate to have known three exceptional women whom I count as true friends. They each
had a powerful and positive impact on my life, and they
continue to influence me in ways I am still discovering.
Each of them faced devastating illness with a bravery I
cannot imagine. I miss each one of them every single
day. This book is dedicated to their memories.

Ellen May Swanson was one of the finest human
beings I will ever know. When I needed a friend, Ellen
was always there. When I lived in Brazil and was unsure
if I could teach quilting, Ellen encouraged me to do so.
When I was considering if I should buy the shop, Ellen
helped me to honestly evaluate the possibilities and
consequences. She literally never said an unkind word
about anyone and firmly believed we can always find
something good in any person or situation, if we are only
willing to look for it.

Esther Jarratt was a friend with whom I shared a
classroom and team-taught third grade. Esther recog-
nized the importance of developing a love for learning
better than anyone I have ever met. She understood that
if a student's needs are met, that student will learn. The
joy and satisfaction we shared in fitting the instruction
to the student, rather than the student to the class, was
the best kind of success. She was the consummate
teacher.

Anna-Marie Griesheimer was my landlady when I
lived and taught in the Netherlands. Mrs. G lived the
kind of life that is chronicled in books. She left Ger-
many in the late 1930s, fought in the Dutch Under-
ground during World War II, and was captured by the
Nazis and sent to a POW camp. She taught me to never
be afraid to do what I know is right, and that "life is too
short to be little."

Acknowledgments

Have you ever read this section of a book and wondered how the list got so long? I finally figured it out. It's because writing a book is such an undertaking that it is impossible to do it without help, and lots of it. I hardly know where to begin, but my heartfelt thanks go to:

Lenore Parham for writing the instructions for Ellen's quilt. From the beginning, she offered encouragement on this project. Lenore backed it up with a lot of hard work when, at the end, I suddenly realized that I needed proofs of yardage and didn't have the foggiest idea how to do them. In addition, Lenore was my personal-computer help person when computer-illiterate me zigged instead of zagged.

Mary Hartman, my trusty administrative assistant. She helped with the proofreading and kept the shop afloat when I was sequestered at the computer for weeks on end.

Laurie Jensen, who did all the decorative illustrations, even though she also happened to be moving across country about the same time I needed them.

The makers of the fabulous quilts within these pages: Jennifer Heffernan, Judy House, Laurie Jensen, Brenda Jones, Kay Lettau, Carolyn Lynch and the Dirty Dozen, and Ellen Swanson. You are pretty heady company for the likes of me.

My incomparable staff, whom I lovingly call "The Troops": Judy Babb, Bonnie Campbell, Alice Crampton, Vera DeWeese, Jill Fath, Sandy Gilchrist, Lesly-Claire Greenberg, Jennifer Heffernan, Judy House, Brenda Jones, Kay Lettau, Carolyn Lynch, Carole Nicholas, Carol Peters, Sue Purdon, Kaye Rhodes, Kathryn Sheehan, Rosemary Tremba, Pat Turley, Rob Vejdani, Nancy Wakefield, and Terri Willett, the absolute best in the world at making The Quilt Patch a gathering place for quilters.

Rosemary Tremba, who supplied a long list of helpful hints, which are interspersed throughout the book, and who quilted my quilt at zero hour.

Carole Deakin of the Fairfax County Parks and Recreation Department, The Bailiwick Inn Bed and Breakfast, and the Fairfax County Courthouse, for allowing us to take photographs.

Our wonderful, gracious, and faithful customers and students, who venture across our threshold every day to share their projects with us and who allow us to do what we love most—surround ourselves with quilts, fabrics, and quilting camaraderie. My special thanks to all of you.

My children, Amanda and Christopher, who have each made a little quilt, becoming the sixth generation of quilters in our family. They were patient most of the time, caring all of the time, and they fill my days with love and sunshine.

Contents

Quilt Patch Tidbits 4
The Quilt Patch and Me 6
Fabric and Supplies 8

Quiltmaking Techniques 9

Making Templates 9
Marking and Cutting Fabric 10
Stitching the Pieces Together 10
Learning to Rotary Cut 12
Pressing 13
Experimenting with Appliqué 13
Adding Borders 15
Marking the Quilt Top 16
Preparing the Quilt Sandwich 17
Quilting Your Quilt 18
Binding Your Quilt 19
Signing Your Quilt 20

The Projects

Midnight Stars 21
Passport to the Amazon 24
Aldora Quilt 28
Lotus Dancer 32
Vermont Star Party 35
Stars Over the Mountains 38
New Horizons 47
Stellafane '90 53
Riot of Roses 61
Elephants That March to a
Different Drummer 67
Escaping the Herd 74
Connected Salzburgs 87

Quilt Patch Tidbits

At the shop we feature tidbits of fabrics, which are really fat eighths. We'd like to share with our readers some other tidbits of information about the shop, but without the fat.

Old Town Fairfax was established in 1805; it played an important role in the history of Northern Virginia. The entire area is littered with history. Mount Vernon, Woodlawn, and Old Town Alexandria are nearby. Williamsburg and Monticello can be reached in a morning's drive. If you have an interest in Civil War history, the Manassas Battlefield, Sully Plantation, and Leesburg are on our doorstep. Historical places are great reasons to visit our area, and they give your family something to do while you visit The Quilt Patch.

Northern Virginia and its surrounding communities in Maryland and the District of Columbia have an active and ever-growing network of quilting guilds. One of the largest is Quilters' Unlimited here in Virginia. With nearly 1,000 members, QU is divided into eleven chapters, with both evening and daytime meetings so everyone can find a group to meet their needs. In addition to regular guild meetings, QU chapters offer bees, workshops, guest speakers, charity and community projects, as well as good quiltmaking and companionship. It is actively engaged in educating school children and the general public about the importance of quiltmaking in the lives of generations of women. The Quilters' Unlimited Annual Show features more than 350 quilts, quilted garments, and cloth dolls. Nor is this the only guild nearby! Cabin Branch Quilters in Virginia, Friendship Star Quilters in Maryland, and The Needlechasers in the District of Columbia are among many other active and exciting groups of quilters in our area. By the way, we honor any dated quilt-guild membership card from anywhere in the world with a 10% discount. You only have to ask.

Is it any wonder that The Quilt Patch is happy to be in the middle of such activity? The multitalented women who comprise these groups need a place to play, and we love being that playground! Every year The Quilt Patch brings in well-known authors, quiltmakers, and dollmakers from around the United States and overseas to complement our own extraordinary teachers. More than half of us have worked on the Jinny Beyer Hilton Head Seminar staff. You won't have the *whoosh, whoosh* of waves outside your window as you quilt, but many of the classes are the same.

The Q.P. Dolls and their "Children"

The Q. P. Dolls is a group that developed out of our doll classes. These dollmakers meet four times a year to hear a program of interest, to exchange ideas, and to introduce other members to their "children." Anyone with an interest in dolls, cloth dolls in particular, is welcome to attend. Things can get a little rowdy when the dollmakers are in, but there isn't another group that has quite the same fun that these intrepid ladies enjoy.

Another great group is known, for lack of a better title, as the Block Exchange Group. These quilters meet once a month to receive a pattern and piece of fabric, which they take home to make into a block. Each month the group holds a

The Block Exchange Group

drawing, and one of the participants in the project wins the blocks. That individual finishes the top. When it is complete, the quilt hangs in The Quilt Patch as the sample for the free Block of the Month pattern, which we hand out to every customer. We have friends who have collected every block since we began the Block of the Month in July 1989.

Mystery Nite is a favorite class that meets every other month on a Friday night, from 7:00 P.M. to midnight. Participants bring food to share and all their stuff, ready for an evening of fun and suspense. The project is almost always an original design by the instructor and often remains a mystery up until the last step, when things suddenly line up and there's the pattern. If students spend more time eating and talking than sewing, we have a Mystery Ketchup Nite so they can finish their projects at a later date.

The Quilt Patch also loans classroom space to quilt guilds that wish to meet monthly to baste their quilts with some help from their friends. One group from the Annandale chapter of QU has been meeting here regularly for several years. That's a lot of basting.

The Annandale QU Basters

The Quilt Patch and Me

It was twenty years ago that Joe and Lu Hildenbrand expanded their needlework shop, The Tapestry Room, and opened The Quilt Patch. They did so at the urging of several women who were part of the Virginia quilt revival in the early 1970s. Hazel Carter, who later founded The Continental Quilting Congress, was particularly instrumental in this endeavor. She worked to form a nucleus of staff members and teachers, some of whom still work and teach at The Quilt Patch.

The original shop made its home in an old one-room schoolhouse in Old Town Fairfax. The building had certainly seen better days, and there was no air-conditioning or even indoor plumbing. It was not uncommon to occasionally see a note pinned to the front door that read "Back in 5 Minutes," while someone dashed up to The Tapestry Room to use the powder room.

It was to this little shop I ventured one day, after taking the first session of a beginning quilt class through the local county adult education

Leslie Anne Pfeifer

Seated: Mary Hartman, Terri Willett, Pat Turley, Brenda Jones, Lesly-Claire Greenberg, Vera DeWeese, Leslie Pfeifer, Jill Fath, and Carole Nicholas. Standing: Bonnie Campbell, Judy House, Judy Babb, Carolyn Lynch, Carol Peters, Kathryn Sheehan, Kay Lettau, Kaye Rhodes, Laurie Jensen, Rosemary Tremba, Nancy Wakefield, and Jennifer Heffernan.

program. The teacher worked part time at The Quilt Patch and suggested I might find supplies and good help there. It was true, and in a short time the ladies of The Quilt Patch became my friends. Not only could I find my tools and fabrics, but the shop became a place where I enjoyed a feeling of contentment. If I had a bad day, I often went to "The Patch" to see Ellen Swanson and my other newfound friends. Just being there improved my day and probably my attitude!

Quiltmaking grew in Northern Virginia, and eventually The Quilt Patch outgrew its small space and traded places with The Tapestry Room (the shop with the bathroom)! When I returned from overseas in 1987, I discovered that the two shops were now under one roof. I asked for work and was promptly hired. They expressed particular interest in whether I could work the next Sunday at the annual outdoor Sully Plantation Quilt Show and Sale. Sully is the site of one of the largest quilting events in the area. It is held on the second Sunday of September on the plantation grounds. I wouldn't miss it!

I went to work on Saturdays with Jennifer Heffernan. By this time, Joe and Lu were think-

ing of retirement and within the year asked if I might be interested in purchasing the shop. It was more like the adoption of a child that needed a little more raising, if a suitable "parent" could be found. Jennifer proved to be invaluable in helping me organize this endeavor, and I bought the shop in 1989.

My goals for The Quilt Patch have always been quite simple. I wanted it to become a gathering place for quilters, a place they could come for help, support, and the friendship of other quilters. I wanted them to learn as much as we could teach, and to enjoy a love of quiltmaking. Next, I needed to provide them with everything they needed to make a quilt of which they could be proud.

What makes The Quilt Patch special? Oh, more than 2,000 bolts of fabric, nearly 1,000 book titles, and all the other stuff is great. But nearly any shop can provide that. I believe the most important thing we do is teach—not just classes, but every day in every way with any quilter who needs help. My staff and teachers are the best. And they are the greatest friends in the world.

Fabric and Supplies

Fabric

At The Quilt Patch we sell only 100% cotton fabrics. Cotton is easy to work with, holds its shape, and generally is predictable. Occasionally a particular garment, handbag, or quilt requires another type of fabric. Sometimes you feel you mustn't waste the yards of leftover fabric from the new slipcovers. We understand your dilemma, but encourage you to use cotton in your quilts. It's not because we want to sell you fabric, but because we want your quiltmaking to be fun. Using the right fabrics makes quiltmaking easier and therefore more enjoyable.

We are fabric lovers at heart, so selecting materials for a quilt is one of the things we love most at The Quilt Patch. Helping to plan quilts with our customers allows us to "make" lots of quilts we'll never find time for in this life.

Unless you are working in all solid colors, look for your focus fabric first, usually a multicolored print. Select supporting fabrics in a variety of scales (size of prints) and values (light, medium, and dark). One fabric should serve as an accent, another as a background. Try to mix prints,

geometric designs, plaids, and stripes (we are especially proud of our selection), and consider the many tone-on-tone prints that we like to call "textured solids." These work well as solids in a quilt, but give a hint of texture rather than the flat look of a plain color. Decorative quilting designs show up well on textured-solid fabrics.

Thread

We feel strongly about the importance of using 100% cotton thread whenever possible. Many of us were home sewers first and used polyester thread because of its strength. It seems like a good idea to use strong thread in our quilts, particularly when it says "cotton covered." Remember, however, that the thread should not be stronger than your fabric. If the quilt gets a lot of use (kid's quilts and quilts headed for college, for instance), it's easier to repair a seam than to fix a hole in the quilt because the thread wouldn't "give" with the fabric. Also, polyester thread can melt when you press your blocks if your heat setting is too high.

Tools

All of us need to watch our spending, but it is important to purchase the best materials and supplies you can afford. Your quilt represents your time, patience, creativity, and in some cases, sacrifice. Don't shortchange your efforts. I once bought a small rotary-cutting mat because I thought the large one was too expensive. It immediately seemed *too* small, so I bought a larger one, which also was really too small. In the end I had purchased two mats I didn't use, which cost more than the large one I passed up in the first place! Remember, your efforts are worth the price of good tools.

Ask your quilt shop to recommend the tools that are basic. For instance, we suggest a particular rotary ruler that has great versatility and value for your investment. We can recommend other tools when you are ready for additional equipment. Many tools today are redundant and may be unnecessary, so inventory what you have and ask for advice.

Quiltmaking Techniques

Making Templates

You need to make cutting templates for some of the quilts in this book. You may cut templates from stiff plastic by tracing the pattern pieces directly onto the plastic. Cut them out with old, sharp scissors—not your fabric-cutting scissors! Another method is to lay the plastic over the pattern, place a ruler along the pattern lines, and score the plastic with an X-Acto™ or craft knife. You don't have to actually cut through the plastic, just slight pressure will do. When you have scored around the pattern piece on all sides, bend the plastic and the template will snap out. This saves time and is more accurate, although you may wish to practice a little first.

Templates for appliqué do not include seam allowances. Templates for machine piecing include the 1/4"-wide seam allowances all around. If you prefer to hand piece, make the templates the finished size of the pattern pieces, without the 1/4"-wide seam allowances.

Hand piecing template

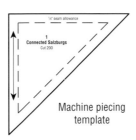

Machine piecing template

Note: The templates for Elephants That March to a Different Drummer, Escaping the Herd, and Stellafane '90 do not include seam allowances.

Mark the pattern name, piece number, and grain-line arrow on the template. You will use the grain-line arrow when placing the template on the fabric. Gently tug on your fabric to find the grain line. The least "give" or stretch is along the straight of grain, the cross grain has a small

amount of stretch, and the bias grain stretches considerably. Match the grain-line arrow on the template to the threads of your fabric, either crosswise or lengthwise. Try to align the edges of pieces that will be on the outside edges of the block or quilt with the straight of grain. This minimizes stretching, making matching corners and seam lines easier.

Marking and Cutting Fabric

Cut away the fabric selvages before cutting out the pieces for your quilt. Place each template face down on the wrong side of the fabric, aligning the grain-line arrow on the template with the straight threads of the fabric. Trace around the template with a pencil. Whenever possible, use a #2 pencil or a mechanical pencil. If you use a dark fabric, a silver, white, or colored pencil may be helpful. Keep the pencil sharp and hold it at an angle, drawing the side of the lead along the edge of the template rather than the point. This prevents some of the "drag" that occurs as you press and move the pencil along on the fabric. If the fabric bunches up, just lift the pencil, let the fabric smooth out, and continue marking. Be sure to leave at least 1/2" between each piece so you have room to add seam allowances.

To mark pieces for hand piecing, trace slightly beyond the corners of the template so that seam intersections are clearly marked.

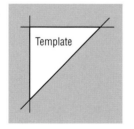

Template

Hand piecing template

After tracing a finished-size template onto the fabric, add a 1/4"-wide seam allowance all around the shape. For shapes with straight sides, place the 1/4" line on your ruler on the drawn seam line and trace along the ruler edge. Carefully cut out the pieces on the outside cutting line.

You may use a rotary cutter instead of marking the cutting line. Place the 1/4" line of your rotary ruler on the marked seam line and rotary cut along the edge of the ruler.

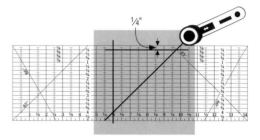

Stitching the Pieces Together

Arrange the pieces on a flat surface the way they will look in your quilt or block. Whenever possible, sew in straight lines and assemble pieces into units or rows that can be sewn together into larger units or rows.

Hand Piecing

When you piece by hand you can take your work with you and put in a few stitches anywhere—at soccer practice or at the doctor's office. It is also relaxing and peaceful, which is a blessing to be enjoyed in today's hurry-up-and-wait world.

To hand stitch two pieces, place them right sides together, matching the edges. Insert a pin through the marked corner of the top piece and check to be sure it comes out through the marked corner on the back piece. Repeat at the other end of the seam. Align the marked seam lines on the pieces and pin them together in the center.

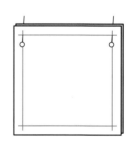

To sew the seam, use a single length of sewing thread no longer than 18". *Do not use quilting thread.* Make a small knot at one end of the thread. Remove the first pin and insert the needle into the exact spot where the pin had been. Sew along the pencil line. Use a running stitch, taking 3 to 4 stitches on the needle.

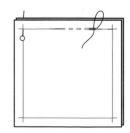

As you stitch, and before you pull your needle through the fabric, check the pencil line on the back piece to make sure you haven't missed it. If you find that you did, slide the needle back a couple of stitches, align the pieces, and sew them again. If the stitches are exactly on the line on both sides, pull the needle through. This saves unthreading your needle and rethreading to remove stitches that are not on the line. Take a single backstitch and continue sewing along the line, stopping at the seam intersection. Do not sew into the seam allowance. Take a single backstitch, make a loop, slip the needle through, and pull to secure the thread.

As you sew units together there will be seams that meet and, occasionally, seams on one side but not on the other. Whenever possible, sew with the unit having the most seams facing you. Never stitch down the seam allowances when piecing by hand. To keep seams tight and secure, as you approach an intersecting seam, make a small backstitch right before the seam allowance. Then bring the needle and thread through the seam and take another backstitch on the other side of the seam.

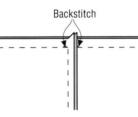

Backstitch

Hand Piecing by Machine

Many quilters like to use their sewing machines to do patchwork, sew appliqué blocks together, or attach sashing and borders. At the shop we teach "hand piecing by machine." With this method, you make individual templates, which include seam allowances, for each piece. You then sew a block together exactly as you would by hand, beginning and ending all stitching at seam intersections.

Before you sew, determine whether your machine has a presser foot that measures exactly ¼" from the stitching line to the right edge of the foot. If so, use the edge of the foot to guide the fabric as you feed it into the machine. If you do not have a ¼" presser foot, you have several options.

❖❖ If your machine has a needle-position control, try moving the needle left or right to make the seam allowance exactly ¼" wide.

❖❖ Take an accurate ruler and slide it under the needle. Using your hand on the machine

wheel, gently lower the needle until it rests precisely on the ¼" line of your ruler. Lay masking tape along the edge of the ruler. Use the tape as a guide for feeding fabric through the machine.

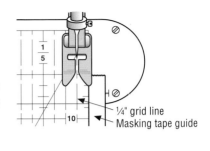

¼" grid line
Masking tape guide

❖❖ There are generic ¼" piecing feet available for most machines, as well as magnetic and adhesive seam guides.

Caution: If you have a computerized sewing machine, do not use magnetic devices on your machine.

I find it essential to watch the ¼" sewing guide in front of the needle rather than at the needle itself. Once the fabric is under the needle, it's too late to adjust.

When you join two pieced units together, press seam allowances in opposite directions so that they butt up against each other. This reduces bulk and makes it easier to match seams.

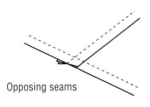

Opposing seams

Place an "indicator" pin in the exact spot where the seams should meet. Pin securely on either side of the indicator pin, catching the seam allowances. You may remove the indicator pin at this point, or leave it until you are a stitch or two away from it and then remove it. Some people are comfortable sewing over the pins. I prefer to remove them because there is usually so much thickness at these intersections.

Chain Piecing

Use a short stitch (twelve to fifteen stitches per inch). Sew the first set of pieces from cut edge to cut edge. At the end of the seam, stop sewing but don't cut the thread. Instead, feed the next set of pieces into the machine right after the first one. If you have a "needle down" feature on your machine, this is a great place to use it.

Continue feeding pieces into the machine without cutting the thread. When all the pairs are sewn together, clip the threads between them and press. I love not having to trim all the long thread tails from starting and stopping!

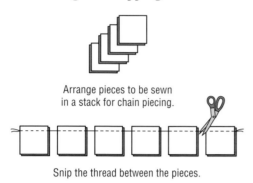

Arrange pieces to be sewn
in a stack for chain piecing.

Snip the thread between the pieces.

Learning to Rotary Cut

Rotary cutting can make quiltmaking faster, easier, and more accurate. With rotary-cutting and strip-piecing methods, you cut strips, cross-cut them into squares or other units, sew the units together into strips, then sew the strips together into the completed quilt top. Often, you do not sew together a block at all.

Here are a few hints from Rosemary Tremba, who teaches most of our rotary classes:

❖❖ If you wash your fabric, use spray sizing (not spray starch) while ironing to put body back into it for easier cutting and sewing. (Also, because all marking will be on top of the sizing, it will come off more easily.)

❖❖ Iron with the grain of the fabric to eliminate distortion.

❖❖ Hold the cutter in the palm of your hand with your index finger on the ridges to minimize wrist and hand strain.

❖❖ Place the palm of your hand on the ruler with your fingers bent and your little finger over the edge to help stabilize the ruler.

❖❖ Be careful. Rotary-cutting blades are extremely sharp.

❖❖ Clean your rotary cutter often, and put a tiny drop of sewing machine oil on the blade. It will lengthen the life of the blade. Always take the cutter apart carefully and lay the pieces down in the order in which you removed them so that you can put them back in reverse order.

❖❖ Measure three times, cut once, and if you do make a mistake, it's only fabric! Relax and let the equipment save you time, not give you gray hair!

Cutting Strips

1. Fold the fabric in half lengthwise with selvage edges together. Fold again into quarters.
2. Position the fabric on the cutting mat with the lengthwise fold next to you and the uneven edges to the right. (Reverse direction if you are left handed.) Line up the edge of a 6" x 24" ruler with the fold. Trim the uneven edge.

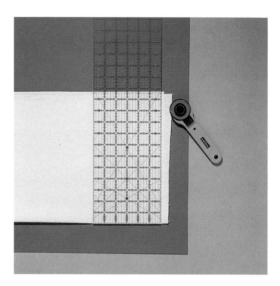

3. Reposition the fabric on the mat (or turn the mat with the fabric 180°) so that the clean-cut edge is on the left. Align the required measurement on the ruler with the cut edge of the fabric and cut the strip.

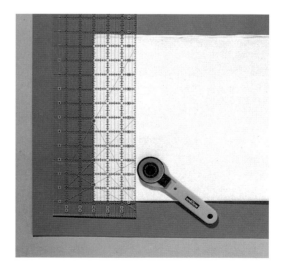

4. After making 3 or 4 cuts, realign the fabric and trim any uneven edges.

Cutting Squares and Rectangles

1. Cut strips of the required width.
2. Line up the correct measurement on the ruler with the left edge of the strip, and cut the size square or rectangle you need. Continue cutting across the strip.

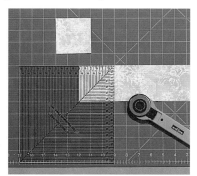

Cutting Half-Square Triangles

1. Cut a square that is ⅞" larger than the *finished short side* of the triangle you need.
2. Cut the square once diagonally to yield 2 half-square triangles.

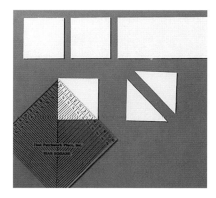

Cutting Quarter-Square Triangles

1. Cut a square that is 1¼" larger than the *finished long side* of the triangle you need.
2. Cut the square twice diagonally to yield 4 quarter-square triangles.

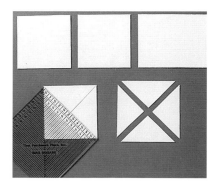

Pressing

Press each seam to one side before adding another piece. You may "finger-press" as you sew, and then press the blocks when you are ready to sew them all together. Do not press seams open unless specifically instructed to do so. We recommend a dry iron because steam can stretch the fabrics if the iron is moved along the pieces. Try to simply press down on the block, picking the iron up to move it rather than ironing back and forth. If possible, press seams toward the darker fabric to prevent them from shadowing through the lighter fabric, but also consider bulky areas and press to evenly distribute the thickness of seam allowances.

Experimenting with Appliqué

Freezer-Paper Appliqué

There are many ways to appliqué. We teach twelve different methods in one of our most popular classes at the shop. Anne Oliver taught me freezer-paper appliqué when I first learned to quilt in 1981. Experiment with as many ways as you can learn, and find what works best for you. This remains the easiest and fastest way for me.

1. Trace each pattern shape onto the dull, uncoated side of a piece of freezer paper. Cut out the shape on the drawn line. Do not add seam allowances.
2. Lightly iron the shapes, shiny side down, onto the right side of your fabric. Use the tip of the iron and tap the paper down in a few places just to hold it in place. Use a dry iron on the cotton setting.

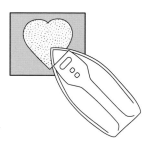

3. Cut out the fabric shapes, adding a ¹/₄"-wide seam allowance all around each one. Allow a little extra for those edges that will lie under another shape.

4. Remove the freezer paper and place it on the wrong side of the fabric shape, shiny side facing up.

Shiny side of freezer paper

Back side of fabric

5. Using the tip and side of the iron, press the seam allowance to the freezer paper. Use a sweeping motion with the side of the iron. If you get a glitch, unstick the freezer paper from the seam allowance with your fingernail and fix it. The paper will stick again. *Do not iron down seam allowances that another piece will cover.* Clip inside points almost to the paper before ironing the seam allowances down. For points, press the seam allowance over the point toward the center of the piece, then press down the sides next to the point to produce a sharp point and no raw edges. You do not need to clip outside curves.

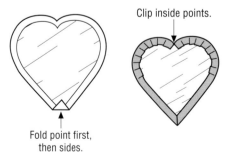

Clip inside points.

Fold point first, then sides.

6. When all the seam allowances are ironed down, position the appliqués on your background fabric in the numerical order of the pattern pieces. When everything is in place, press the entire appliqué design with your iron. It will stick, although at this point I usually put in a pin or two just to be sure the pieces don't slip out of place.

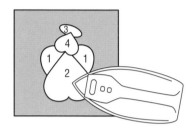

7. Using a small blind stitch and a single thread that matches the fabric being appliquéd, sew the appliqué shapes to the background. Start the first stitch from the back of the block. Bring the needle through the background and catch the very edge of the appliqué piece. You should feel the paper with your needle and come up through only the fabric. Insert the needle into the background right next to where you brought it up, then bring the needle up through both layers of fabric approximately ¹/₈" from the first stitch.

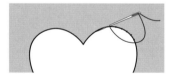

8. Sew around all the appliqué shapes. If a piece is on top of another, the bottom piece becomes the "background" for the top piece. When this happens, begin stitching by bringing the needle up through the edge of the top piece and pushing the knot under the piece to hide it. If you finish sewing around a piece that lies on top of another piece, make a knot in the thread as if you were hand quilting. Take the last stitch and gently tug the knot through the fabric to hide it.

9. When all the pieces are appliquéd in place, turn the work over. You will see the stitches outlining the appliqué. With small, sharp

scissors, cut ¼" inside the stitching line and remove the excess fabric. With your fingernail, gently unstick the freezer paper from the seam allowance and remove it. You will see the outlines of other pieces appliquéd on top. Remove each layer in the same manner until all the freezer paper is gone.

Machine Appliqué

Make a paper template without seam allowances for each shape. Pin them to the right side of the fabric. Cut out the pieces, without adding seam allowances. Use a water-soluble glue stick to hold pieces in position on the background fabric. Sew around each piece using a short, narrow zigzag stitch, blanket stitch, or buttonhole stitch.

Fusible Appliqué

There are certain projects we all wish to make, but have difficulty justifying the time required; especially, perhaps, for a seasonal piece that will only hang for a few weeks every year. That's when paper-backed fusible web is handy.

1. Trace the pattern shapes onto the paper side of the fusible web, keeping in mind that they will be reversed when you are finished. Trace the pattern in reverse, using a light box or a bright window.

2. Cut the pieces apart ¼" outside the lines you traced. Following the manufacturer's directions, fuse them to the wrong sides of your fabrics.

3. Cut out the fabric appliqué pieces along the traced lines on the fusible web. Remove the paper backing and position the pieces on your background fabric. Following the manufacturer's directions, fuse them to the background. Machine stitch around the appliqués, buttonhole stitch around them by hand, leave them alone, or use a permanent-ink fabric marker with a very fine point to draw little stitch lines around each piece.

It's a good idea to store fused appliqué projects by rolling them up rather than folding. They should be around to brighten your seasons for years to come.

Adding Borders

Not every quilt "wants" a border, and sometimes a quilt particularly doesn't want one made out of the fabric you purchased when you first set out to make it. This is why we often recommend that you wait to buy the border fabric until the top has been completed. You can then "interview" fabric for the position of honor. Often a quilt has a mind of its own, and it turns out lighter, darker, or more purple than you thought it would. If that is the case, you can adjust by careful border treatment.

Always measure your quilt in both directions across the middle, not along the edges. The edges may have stretched during sewing and handling. Using distorted quilt-edge measurements gives you wavy, uneven borders. Measuring across the middle helps to "square up" the quilt because stretched edges can be eased in along the length of the border strip.

The quilt patterns in this book include the correct measurements for the quilt border strips. They will fit your quilt if your piecing is perfect. In real life our seams sometimes vary from perfection, so at The Quilt Patch we recommend cutting border strips longer than necessary, then trimming them when you are ready to add them to the quilt.

Plain Borders

1. Measure the length of your quilt across the center from the top edge to the bottom edge. Cut two border strips to that measurement and sew them to the sides of the quilt, using a ¼"-wide seam allowance.

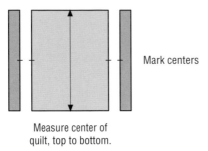

Mark centers

Measure center of
quilt, top to bottom.

2. Measure the width of the quilt across the middle from side edge to side edge, including the side borders just added. Cut two border strips to that exact measurement. Sew them to the top and bottom of the quilt, matching centers and ends.

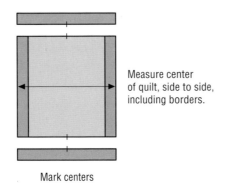

Measure center
of quilt, side to side,
including borders.

Mark centers

Borders with Mitered Corners

To frame your quilt with mitered corners, measure the length and width of the quilt across the center, adding twice the width of the borders plus seam allowances to each strip before cutting. (Cut the border strips 2 to 3 inches longer than needed just to be safe.)

1. Mark the center points of the border strips, and mark half of the exact length of the quilt top on either side of the center with pencil marks in the border seam allowances.

Center of border strip

Length of quilt at center

2. If you are adding multiple borders, sew all border strips together first and miter them all at the same time.

3. Using a ¼"-wide seam allowance, sew a border strip to each side of the quilt, matching centers and corners with the marks in the border seam allowances. Start and stop your stitching ¼" from each edge. Press seams toward the border.

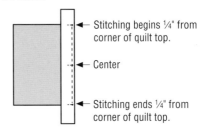

← Stitching begins ¼" from corner of quilt top.

← Center

← Stitching ends ¼" from corner of quilt top.

4. Lay a corner of the quilt top on your ironing board or work table, keeping it as flat as possible. Fold one of the border strips under at a 45° angle, matching seams or stripes exactly.

5. Pin, checking the corner to ensure that it is perfectly square. Press the fold. You may choose to hand stitch the fold down at this point.

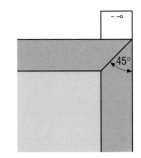

45°

6. Turn the quilt over and draw a line on the crease or fold line. Align the long edges of the border strips and stitch on the pencil line. Trim the excess fabric and press. Repeat for the other corners.

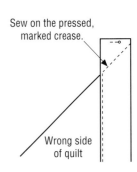

Sew on the pressed, marked crease.

Wrong side of quilt

Marking the Quilt Top

Many quilters mark their quilt tops for quilting before putting the three layers together. Use a mechanical pencil with fabric lead, a washable graphite pencil, or a colored-chalk pencil to draw the quilting lines.

You may also choose to mark the top as you quilt. At The Quilt Patch, we like to use $1/4$"-wide masking tape for straight outline quilting, but remember to remove it immediately after quilting so no residue remains on the fabric. Another great marking tool is a chalk pencil or wheel. The chalk brushes off after quilting. It must be applied just before you stitch, because the lines rub away so easily with handling. The advantage, of course, is that there is no need to wash your quilt to remove lines later on. It is always a good idea to test your marking tool on a scrap of each fabric from your project to make sure the lines can be removed easily.

Preparing the Quilt Sandwich

The quilt sandwich is composed of the pieced or appliquéd quilt top, batting, and backing. Cut or assemble your backing so that it is a minimum of 2" larger than the top on all sides. (Count on 42" of usable fabric width due to shrinkage and removal of the selvage edges.) If you must sew two or more lengths together to cover the back, use a single full-width panel for the center and divide the remaining length into two narrow pieces. Sew a piece to each side of the center panel. This eliminates stress on a single center seam. Press the seams to the sides.

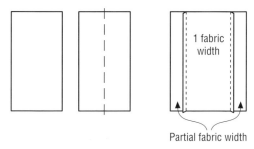

1 fabric width

Partial fabric width

Batting is the filler of the quilt sandwich. There are many types on the market today and everyone has a favorite. If you are a beginning quilter, try one of the lightweight polyester battings. As you develop your quilting skills, experiment with other types of batting. The new wool battings are soft, warm, made of natural fiber (like the 100% cotton fabrics), and wonderful to hand quilt. The Quilt Patch sells precut squares of several kinds of batting so quilters can try them out before making a final selection.

Machine quilters usually prefer cotton or cotton-polyester batting because the fabric tends to "stick" to the surface of the batting and there is less shifting. Remove the batting from the bag, unfold it gently, and let it "breathe" for several hours. It will be easier to smooth out wrinkles. Always follow the manufacturer's instructions for preparing the batting. Some require presoaking and drying. Just remember: Never agitate or you will have mush in your washing machine.

1. Place the backing on the floor or on a large table, right side down. Smooth the backing and tape it to the work surface, being careful not to stretch the fabric.
2. Spread the batting over the backing. It should be at least as large as the backing, 2" larger than the quilt top on all sides.
3. Center the quilt top on the batting, smoothing it out from the center. Pin with straight pins around the edge, about every 6 inches.
4. Baste the layers together using a long, thin darning needle and white or light-colored thread. Start in the middle and use long stitches that will be easy to remove later. Baste from the middle to the edge of the quilt in horizontal and vertical lines approximately 6" apart. *Never reverse the direction of the basting stitches. If the quilt top shifts as you quilt from the center, a diagonal or reverse line of basting stops the movement and causes bunching.*
5. At the end of a line of basting, take one or two large back stitches. After basting, remove the pins and tape.

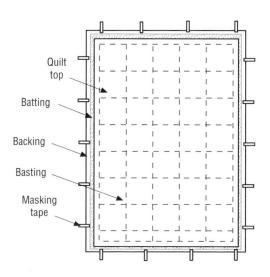

Quilt top

Batting

Backing

Basting

Masking tape

For machine quilting, pin-baste with rust-proof safety pins about every 4" to 6". People often ask if they can pin-baste for hand quilting. We advise against it because, as you quilt, the thread will snag around every safety pin it can find. Safety pins are also difficult to work around with a quilting hoop or frame. If you really wish to pin-baste for hand quilting, try placing the pins on the back of the quilt by reversing the positions of the top, batting, and backing as you assemble the quilt sandwich.

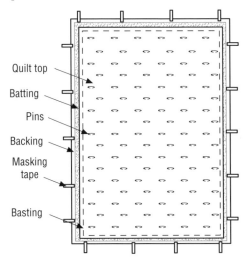

Quilt top
Batting
Pins
Backing
Masking tape
Basting

Pin basting for machine quilting

Quilting Your Quilt

Hand Quilting

Quilting stitches are small running stitches that hold the three layers of the quilt together. More than that, quilting adds dimension and beauty to your quilt and can be an important design element. Do not allow yourself to get discouraged if you aren't able to get twelve stitches to an inch like Great-Aunt Mabel. Concentrate on the evenness of the stitches, so that the spaces between the stitches are the same size as the stitches and the stitches on the back are about the same size as those on the front.

One of our most popular classes spends three sessions dealing with the rudiments of producing perfect quilting stitches, and students still have to practice. Take some time, and don't be too hard on yourself.

1. Tie a small, single knot at the end of an 18"

length of quilting thread. It may be a neutral color, or you may wish to match thread to the fabric. If you plan to change colors, select a multicolored-print backing so that the stitches are not so visible.

2. Insert the needle through the top layer only, about ³/₄" away from where you wish to begin quilting. Slide the needle between the layers and pull it up at your starting point. Give the thread a gentle tug. The knot should pop through the fabric and be hidden in the batting.

3. Make small running stitches, going through all three layers. Take 3 to 4 stitches at a time. A rubber disk or finger cot worn on your thumb helps you pull the needle through if it gets stuck.

4. To end a line of quilting, make a small knot in the thread about ¹/₄" away from the quilt top. Take the final stitch, or a backstitch if you wish. Bring your needle up ³/₄" away from the final stitch and pop the knot into the batting. Clip the thread carefully. This is no time to snip a hole in the fabric!

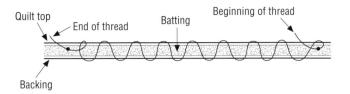

Quilt top
End of thread
Batting
Beginning of thread
Backing

Machine Quilting

We all know we will never have time to make all the quilts we'd like to make, but machine quilting helps by speeding up the quilting process. Besides making quilts more durable (important when they go off to college or get dragged around as a child's favorite "lovey"), machine quilting also adds interest to your quilt.

Once you get the hang of it, try experimenting with metallic and other decorative threads. A very fine nylon "invisible" thread in either clear (for light fabrics) or smoke (for darker fabrics) gives the impression of quilting without all those machine stitches showing. Being a natural-fiber enthusiast, I hesitated to endorse this method, but there's always an exception to the rule. I find that I actually enjoy the dimension achieved by "invisible stitches."

A walking foot is very helpful for quilting straight lines and for basting areas you plan to free-motion quilt. The walking foot is sometimes called an "even-feed foot" because it feeds all layers of the quilt through the machine together, without puckering or shifting.

Walking foot

A darning foot is essential for free-motion quilting. Drop the feed dogs on your machine so that you, not the machine, control the movement of the fabric.

Darning foot

You may "meander" all over the top, following patterns in the fabric, or stipple the background behind an appliqué shape, using tight lines of quilting. Get in the habit of looking ahead to where you are going so that your hands have time to react. Learn to watch the fabric in front of the needle, not at the needle itself. Remember, when you start to sew, pull the bottom thread up through the quilt, and hold on to both threads to prevent them from tangling on the bottom of the quilt.

Hold onto threads where you start.

Free Motion Quilting

Binding Your Quilt

Note: If your quilt has rounded corners, like Lotus Dancer, page 32, or sharply angled edges, like Vermont Star Party, page 35, use single bias binding. Cut bias strips 1¹/₂" wide and do not fold in half. Sew the binding to the quilt using a ¹/₄"-wide seam allowance. Turn the binding to the back of the quilt, fold the edge under ¹/₄", and blindstitch in place.

Double bias binding is the longest-wearing finish for the edges of your quilt. Use a walking foot to sew the binding to the quilt. If you don't have a walking foot, baste around the edge of the quilt, either by hand or by machine, before attaching the binding.

Rotary cut 2¹/₄"-wide strips on the bias. Find the true bias of your fabric with a 45° triangle or a ruler with the 45° angle marked.

Sew the ends of the bias strips together to make a continuous strip long enough to go around the edge of the quilt, plus about six extra inches. Turn the strip under ¹/₄" at one end and press. Fold the strip wrong sides together and press.

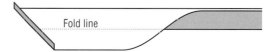

Fold line

1. Align the raw edges of the binding with the edge of the quilt. Sew the binding to the quilt, starting at the center of one side. Stop and backstitch ¹/₄" from the corner.

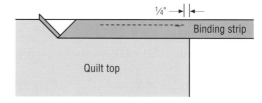

¹/₄"

Binding strip

Quilt top

2. Turn the quilt to sew the next side. Fold the binding back at a 45° angle, then fold straight down along the edge of the quilt. This creates a mitered corner when the binding is turned to the back.

3. Stitch from the edge of the binding fold to the next corner and repeat the procedure.

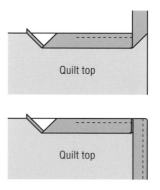

Quilt top

Quilt top

4. When you reach the starting point, cut off the excess binding, leaving enough to tuck in the folded end of the binding, and finish sewing the seam.

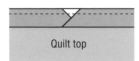

Quilt top

5. Turn the binding to the back of the quilt and blindstitch in place, covering the machine stitching. Tuck in the corners to form miters and blindstitch.

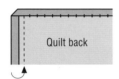

Quilt back

Quilt back

Signing Your Quilt

I now have quilts made by six generations of my family, including three little ones made by my children, now 7 and 9 years old. Fortunately for me, my mother remembered who made which quilt and approximately when. Not everyone is so fortunate. The meaning of many a quilter's legacy was lost because her identity was forgotten. You have put time, effort, and love into your quilt. Finish the job and label it properly with name, date, and place. A label doesn't have to be elaborate. Years from now someone may see your quilt and want to know who made it. Don't make them wonder who you were.

 Quilt Patch Recipe:
Death by Chocolate
Contributed by Tami Jewell

There's a wonderful bakery in Old Town Fairfax called Victoria's Cakery. The cakes and other goodies are truly decadent and Vicky's chocolate cake has qualities that send chocoholics into spasms. We can't hang out at the Cakery every day, and we can't compete with Victoria's cakes, but if you love chocolate, this will make your day.

One 21½-ounce package of brownie mix or a 9" x 13" pan
    of homemade brownies
¼ to ½ cup Kahlua®
Two 3½-ounce packages of chocolate mousse mix,
    prepared according to package directions
12-ounce tub Cool Whip®
8 Heath® bars, crushed
1 cup chopped pecans

Make brownies according to package directions. Cool. Poke holes in the top and pour Kahlua over the top. Crumble the brownies with a fork and put half in the bottom of a large, clear bowl. (A trifle dish works well.) Layer half of the mousse, half of the Cool Whip, half of the Heath bars, and half of the pecans. Repeat the layers. Chill until time to serve.

Midnight Stars

By Ellen Swanson, 1982, Fairfax, Virginia, 35½" x 44½".

Ellen Swanson began working and teaching at The Quilt Patch in 1976. Her first love was teaching beginners, which she did until she was diagnosed with cancer in September 1993. Her knowledge of and devotion to Amish quilts and their makers became her trademark, and this book would not be complete without including one of her many Amish pieces. We lost Ellen in January 1994, but we will never lose her inspiration as a quiltmaker, teacher, and friend.

Materials: 44"-wide fabric

1³/₄ yds. black for background and borders
¹/₂ yd. blue
³/₈ yd. blue-violet
¹/₄ yd. purple
1¹/₂ yds. for backing
¹/₃ yd. for binding
40" x 49" piece of batting

Quilt Patch Pointer: Cut border strips full length on the straight of grain before cutting the block pieces, to ensure seamless borders that are strong, stable, and easy to handle. Cut the border strips a little longer than necessary. Cut each strip to the required size after piecing the top.

Cutting

From the black, cut:
4 strips, each 6¹/₄" x 54", from the lengthwise grain of the fabric.
From the remaining black fabric (approximately 17" x 54"), cut the following strips across the fabric width (crosswise grain). *Label each stack of black pieces with the cut size for easier assembly.*
4 strips, each 6¹/₂" x 17"; crosscut into 8 squares, each 6¹/₂" x 6¹/₂", for piece G.
2 strips, each 3¹/₂" x 17"; crosscut into 4 rectangles, each 3¹/₂" x 6¹/₂", for Unit 1.
4 strips, each 2" x 17"; crosscut into 8 rectangles, each 2" x 6¹/₂", for piece A.
2 strips, each 2" x 17"; crosscut into 6 rectangles, each 2" x 3¹/₂", for Unit 3.
1 strip, 2" x 17"; crosscut into 4 squares, each 2" x 2", for Unit 2.

From the blue fabric, cut:
1 strip, 3¹/₂" x 42"; crosscut into 9 squares, each 3¹/₂" x 3¹/₂", for piece E.
4 strips, each 2" x 42"; crosscut into 72 squares, each 2" x 2", for Units 1, 2, and 3.
From the blue-violet fabric, cut:
2 strips, each 3¹/₂" x 42"; crosscut into 10 rectangles, each 3¹/₂" x 6¹/₂", for Unit 2.

From the purple fabric, cut:
1 strip, 3¹/₂" x 42"; crosscut into 4 rectangles, each 3¹/₂" x 6¹/₂", for Unit 2.

Assembling the Units

1. Fold 2 of the blue 2" x 2" squares diagonally and finger-press.

2. Open a square and place it on one corner of a black 3¹/₂" x 6¹/₂" rectangle, right sides together. Stitch along the fold line as shown.

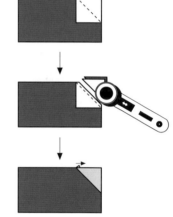

3. Trim the seam allowance to ¹/₄" from the stitching line and press toward the corner.

4. Sew another blue square to the adjacent corner of the rectangle. Trim and press.

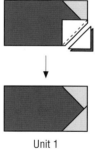

Unit 1
Make 4

5. Using the technique for Unit 1, make the required number of each color combination as shown for Unit 2.

Unit 2   Unit 2   Unit 2
Make 2   Make 8   Make 4

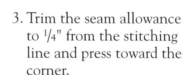

6. Sew 2 blue 2" x 2" squares to each of the 2" x 3½" black rectangles as shown for Unit 3.

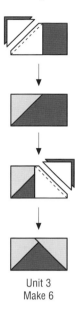

Unit 3
Make 6

Assembling the Quilt Top

1. Arrange the units in 7 rows as shown below.

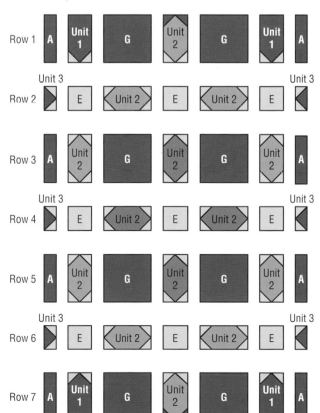

2. Sew the units together in horizontal rows, pressing the seams of the odd-numbered rows in one direction and the seams of the even-numbered rows in the opposite direction.
3. Sew the rows together, taking care to match seams accurately.
4. Referring to "Plain Borders" on page 16, measure the quilt, trim the border strips to the correct sizes, and add the borders to the quilt.

Finishing

1. Using the feather quilting design on the pullout pattern, mark the design on the quilt borders. Use the quilt diagram as a guide to mark the quilting lines for the stars and a ¾" grid for the background. The grid extends into the border "behind" the feathers.

2. Layer the quilt top with batting and backing. Baste the layers together.
3. Quilt as shown, using black thread.
4. Bind and label your Midnight Stars quilt.

Passport to the Amazon

By Leslie A. Pfeifer, 1994, Fairfax,
Virginia, 30$\frac{1}{2}$" x 30$\frac{1}{2}$".

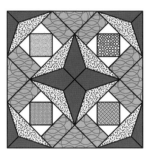

I taught quilting when I lived in Brazil from 1984–1986.
I designed the Imperial Topaz block, naming it for a gem-
stone indigenous to that country. The original quilt was
hand-pieced in 12" blocks.

Later, I decided to put my rotary-cutting skills to work
and came up with a machine-pieced version, assembled in
strips rather than blocks. It was while my son, who was born
in Brazil, was taking a summer safari course entitled
"Passport to the Amazon" at the National Zoo in Washing-
ton, D.C., that I realized how much the colors reminded me
of the brilliant flora and fauna of the Amazon basin.

Materials: 44"-wide fabric

¼ yd. large-scale print
½ yd. red-and-purple print
½ yd. total of assorted black prints
⅛ yd. teal print
¼ yd. pale yellow print
⅝ yd. black print for inner border and binding
½ yd. purple print for outer border
1 yd. for backing
36" x 36" piece of batting

Cutting

Use the templates on the pullout pattern at the back of the book.

From the large-scale print, cut:
32 template C
4 template G
8 template H

From the red-and-purple, cut:
32 template D

From the assorted black, cut:
24 template F
8 template E
8 template E reversed

From the teal, cut:
16 template A

From the pale yellow, cut:
64 template B

From the black inner border and binding fabric, cut:
4 strips, each 1" x 42"

From the purple outer border fabric, cut:
4 strips, each 3" x 42"

Assembling the Units

 Quilt Patch Pointer: When faced with set-in seams, make freezer-paper templates without seam allowances.

1. Trace the template shape without seam allowances onto the dull, uncoated side of a piece of freezer paper. Stack several more pieces of freezer paper beneath the first and cut out multiples of the template, using scissors or a rotary-cutting blade that is too dull for cutting fabric.

2. Iron a freezer-paper template, shiny side down, onto the wrong side of your fabric.

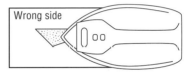
Wrong side

3. Using a rotary-cutting ruler as a guide, cut the fabric ¼" away from the edge of the paper on all sides of the template. Do not remove the paper.

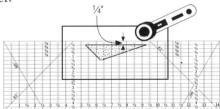
¼"

4. Place the pieces right sides together, matching the points of the paper templates. Sew the seam, using the edge of the paper as a guide. Since the paper is visible as you sew, there is no guessing where to stop and start for setting-in odd-shaped pieces. When you no longer need them for stitching, remove the paper pieces. Reuse them until they are no longer sticky. Let's hear it for freezer paper! I use it as often as possible.

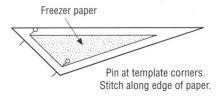
Freezer paper
Pin at template corners.
Stitch along edge of paper.

Unit 1

1. Place a piece E and a piece Er right sides together as shown. Matching the seam intersections, sew from the outer corner to 1/4" from the opposite edge. Backstitch at the marked seam intersection. Finger-press the pieces open.

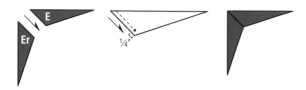

2. With right sides together, sew a piece D to piece E, stitching from the outside corner to the inner point, taking care not to stitch down the seam allowance between pieces E and Er. Stitch the remaining side of piece D to piece Er in the same manner.

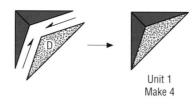

Unit 1
Make 4

3. Gently press the unit, taking care not to stretch the edges.

Unit 2

1. Sew a piece E to a piece F, stopping 1/4" from the edge as shown. Gently finger-press the pieces open.

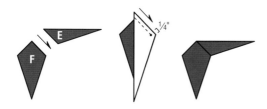

2. Sew a piece Er to the other side of piece F, again stopping 1/4" from the edge. Finger-press the pieces open.

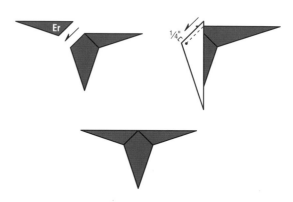

3. To complete the unit, add a piece D to each side, as shown in step 2 for Unit 1. Press the seams away from piece F.

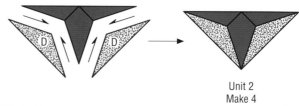

Unit 2
Make 4

Unit 3

1. Sew together 4 of piece F as shown, stitching from the center edges outward and stopping 1/4" from the outer edge of each piece.

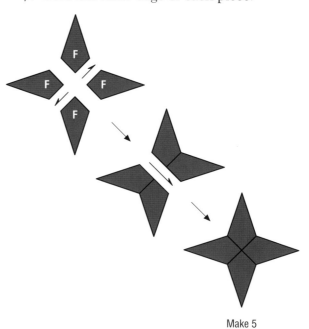

Make 5

2. Add 4 piece D to the resulting unit, stitching from the outer point to the inner seam.

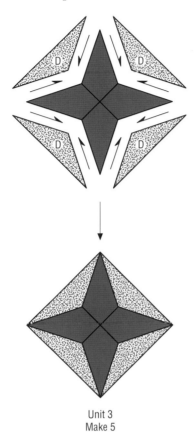

Unit 3
Make 5

Unit 4

1. Sew 4 of piece B to a piece A to make a square within a square as shown.

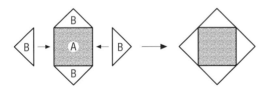

2. Sew a piece C to each end of the square.

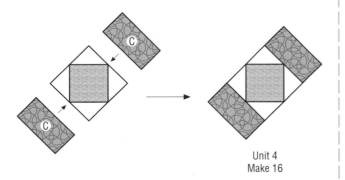

Unit 4
Make 16

Assembling the Quilt Top

1. Arrange the units and pieces G and H in diagonal rows as shown below. Sew the units together, pressing the seams in even-numbered rows in one direction and the seams in odd-numbered rows in the opposite direction.

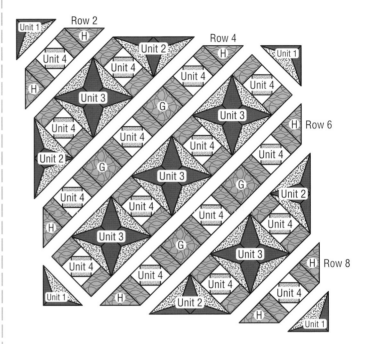

2. Join the rows, carefully matching the seams between the units. Add the 4 corner units (Unit 1) last.
3. Referring to "Plain Borders" on page 16, measure the quilt, trim the inner border strips to the correct sizes, and add them to the quilt.
4. Add the outer border in the same way.

Finishing

1. Layer the quilt top with batting and backing; baste the layers together.
2. Quilt as desired.
3. Bind the edges.
4. Sign and date your quilt.

Aldora Quilt

Designed, assembled, and quilted by Andrea Perkins, 1992, McLean, Virginia, 49¹/₂" x 54¹/₂". Blocks made by friends of Ellen Swanson.

Aldora means "Winged Gift." She is a tiny angel made of hearts who watches over friends in need. These little angels arrive in the mail with signed individual messages of love, hope, and encouragement for a person who is ill or going through a difficult time.

Aldora was originally designed for a friend whose husband was dying. Sometimes Aldora blocks came to her in batches and sometimes alone. Some came long after her husband's death, but every single one carried the message "I care about you."

Quilt Patch Pointer: The Aldora block setting shown here is only a suggestion and was designed to accommodate the number of blocks Ellen received. We encourage you to play with different ways to set your blocks. Aldora is very versatile and happy in any arrangement that pleases you.

Materials: 44"-wide fabric

For One Aldora Block
6" x 6" square for background
3¼" x 3¼" square of print fabric for dress
3¼" x 3¼" square of print fabric for wings
1" x 2" piece of lamé or gold for halo
2" x 2" square of flesh-tone fabric for face/head
Permanent-ink fabric marking pens for face
Pink crayon or blush for cheeks
Freezer paper for templates
Optional: Embroidery floss, paper-backed fusible web, and glitter paint writer

For the Aldora Quilt Shown
½ yd. dark solid for window
½ yd. medium solid for window
⅝ yd. for sashing
⅓ yd. for inner border
1¾ yds. for outer border
3¼ yds. for backing
½ yd. for binding
54" x 59" piece of batting

Cutting

From the background fabric, cut:
4 strips, each 6" x 42". Crosscut into 28 squares, each 6" x 6".

From the dark solid, cut:
6 strips, each 2" x 42". Crosscut into 28 rectangles, each 2" x 7³⁄₈". Use a Bias Square ruler to trim one end of each rectangle at a 45° angle.

From the medium solid, cut:
6 strips, each 2" x 42". Crosscut into 28 rectangles, each 2" x 7³⁄₈". Use a Bias Square ruler to trim each rectangle at a 45° angle.

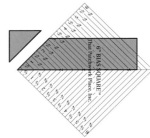

From the sashing fabric, cut:
1 strip, 7" x 42". Crosscut into 24 rectangles, each 1½" x 7".
7 strips, each 1½" x 42"

From the inner border fabric, cut:
5 strips, each 2" x 42"; crosscut into:
2 strips, each 2" x 8"
2 strips, each 2" x 9½"

From the outer border fabric, cut:
4 strips, each 4½" x 58"
2 squares, each 8" x 8"

Making the Aldora Blocks

1. Use the Aldora pattern on page 31. Refer to "Freezer-Paper Appliqué" on pages 13–15 to make templates; cut out each angel piece, leaving a ³⁄₁₆" seam allowance around all sides.
2. Draw the face on the head (piece #4).
3. Appliqué each piece to the background fabric in numerical order.
4. On the back of the appliquéd figure, carefully trim the background fabric ¼" away from the inside of the stitching lines and remove the freezer paper. Measure and trim blocks to 5½" x 5½".
5. Write a message of love, hope, and encouragement in the upper left corner of the block and sign your name at the bottom left edge of the skirt, or wherever you choose.

Quilt Patch Pointer: This is a good project for fusible appliqué as shown on page 15. After you have fused all the pieces in place, finish the edges with a decorative hand or machine stitch or with fabric paint. Make the halo with a glitter paint writer or embroider a ring of French knots.

Framing The Blocks

1. On the wrong side of each block, mark the seam intersection for the lower left corner. This mark will help you miter the window frame.

2. Sew a dark window piece to the left side of each Aldora block, stopping at the marked seam intersection in the bottom left corner.

3. Sew a medium window piece to the bottom of each Aldora block, stopping at the seam intersection in the lower left corner.

   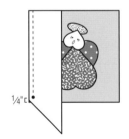

4. Sew the window together along the diagonal edges to create the mitered window frame.

5. Measure and trim the blocks to exactly 7" x 7".

Assembling the Quilt Top

1. Sew 1½" x 7" sashing strips to the right sides of 23 Aldora blocks.

2. For Row 1, sew 3 blocks together. Add a 1½" x 7" sashing strip to the left side of the row. Trim a 1½" x 42" sashing strip to match the exact length of the top row. Sew the strip to the top of Row 1, then trim and add an inner border strip as shown.

   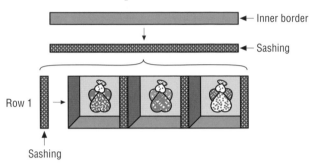

3. Sew a 2" x 8" inner border strip to one side of each of the 8" x 8" border squares. Sew 2" x 9½" inner border strips to the bottoms of these squares. Add the border squares to each end of Row 1.

   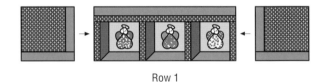

   Row 1

4. For each of the remaining rows, sew 5 Angel blocks together. Use a block with no sashing strip on the right as the last block in each row.

5. Trim 6 sashing strips to the length of the long rows and sew them to the tops of Rows 2–6 and to the bottom of Row 6.

   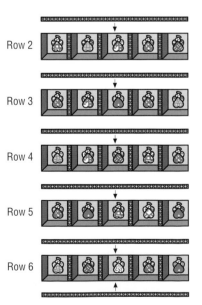

6. Sew Rows 2–6 together. Trim the 2 remaining sashing strips to match the length of the quilt top sides. Sew them to the sides of the quilt. Trim two 2"-wide inner border strips to match the length of the quilt. Sew them to the sides. Trim and sew an inner border strip to the bottom.

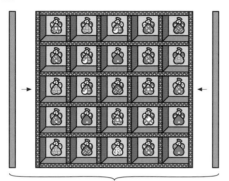

7. Sew Row 1 to the top of the quilt.
8. Referring to "Plain Borders" on page 16, measure the quilt. Trim border strips if needed and add the 4½"-wide outer border strips first to the top and bottom, then to the sides of the quilt.

Finishing the Quilt

1. Layer the quilt top with batting and backing. Baste the layers together.
2. Quilt as desired.
3. Bind the edges of the quilt.
4. Sign, date, and treasure the messages of love and hope.

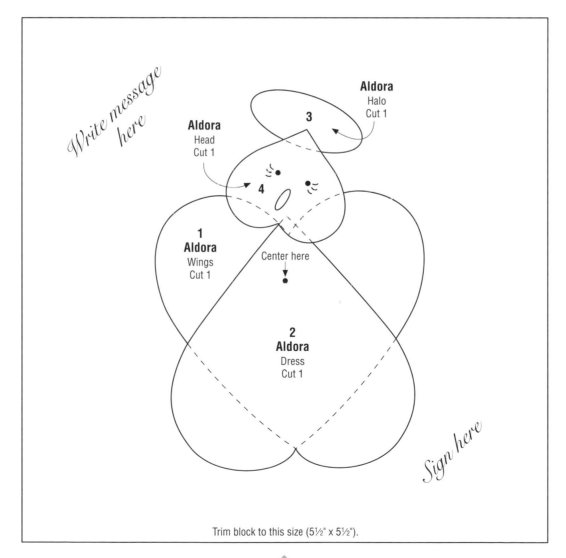

Write message here

Aldora
Halo
Cut 1

3

Aldora
Head
Cut 1

4

1
Aldora
Wings
Cut 1

Center here

2
Aldora
Dress
Cut 1

Sign here

Trim block to this size (5½" x 5½").

Lotus Dancer

By Laurie Jensen, 1992, Fairfax, Virginia, 48" x 51".

After acquiring some wonderful Japanese fabrics and a set of 60° triangle templates of different sizes, Laurie's imagination started working overtime. Her artistic background and innovative approach to quiltmaking allowed her to take a nontraditional look at a very traditional pattern. Laurie used many prints, plaids, and stripes, along with bright, Oriental kimono prints and textured ikats, to produce this contemporary quilt.

Materials: 44"-wide fabric

1 yd. large-scale print focus fabric
2¼ yds. total of assorted coordinating prints
2 strips of border fabric, each 6½" x 53"
3 yds. for backing
½ yd. for binding
53" x 55" piece of batting

Quilt Patch Pointer
Laurie likes to "speed cut":
1. Layer 4 fabrics right sides up in a stack. Place the template on the fabric.
2. Cover the template with a rotary ruler, lining up the edge with the side of the template. Rotary cut 4 triangles at a time, flipping the template after each cut. Make sure that your templates include seam allowances.

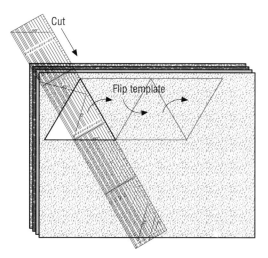

Cutting

Use the templates on the pullout pattern at the back of the book.
From the focus fabric, cut:
16 triangle A

From the coordinating prints, cut:
4 triangle A1
4 triangle A1 reversed
18 triangle B
30 triangle C
502 triangle D

Assembly

Before you begin to sew, consider that this type of quilt evolves during its construction. You may wish to make a few units and assemble them before cutting and sewing more units. A design wall or board is very helpful for arranging them.

1. Sew 4 of triangle D together as shown. Press seams away from the center triangle. All of the pieced triangle units are constructed in this way.

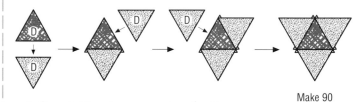

Make 90

2. Sew 3 D units to a triangle C.

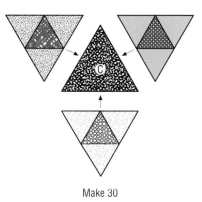

Make 30

3. Sew 3 C/D units to triangle B.

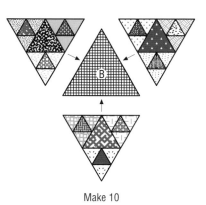

Make 10

4. Arrange the B/C/D units with large A triangles in rows. Begin and end each row with A1 and A1 reversed. Move the units and

triangles around until the colors and patterns please you. Sew the rows together.

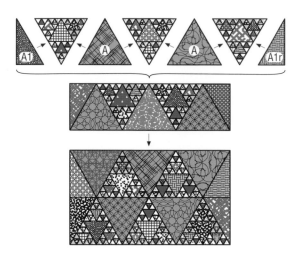

Piecing the Borders

1. Sew 4 of the remaining triangles to 3 of triangle A as shown, beginning and ending with triangle B. Trim the A triangles even with the tops of the B triangles.

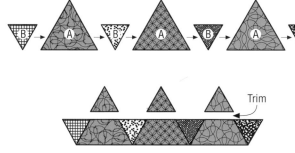

Make 2 strips.

2. Mark a line on each end triangle, dividing it in half. Trim ¼" *outside* the marked line as shown.

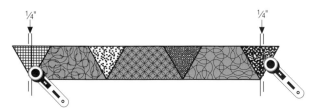

3. Sew the A/B borders to the top and bottom of the quilt as shown below.
4. Sew together 2 strips, each consisting of 71 D triangles.

5. Sew the triangle strips to the sides of the quilt top. Trim them even with the top and bottom.
6. Measure the length of the quilt top through the center. Trim two 6½"-wide border strips to fit. Sew the strips to the sides of quilt top.

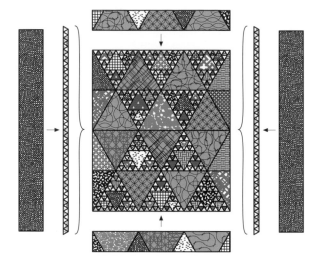

Quilt Patch Pointer:

Laurie appliquéd Japanese family crests in the borders, as well as butterflies overlapping the borders. You can cut motifs from fabric or draw your own crests to appliqué.

Finishing

1. Layer the quilt top with backing and batting. Baste.
2. Quilt as desired. Laurie chose a variety of sashiko designs and randomly quilted them in the larger unpieced areas. She outline-quilted the small pieced triangles.
3. Laurie rounded the corners of her quilt. You can do this easily with a large circle template or dinner plate. Place the circle on the corner and mark around the curve with a pencil. Trim with scissors.
4. Bind the edges with bias-cut binding.
5. Label your quilt and admire the plethora of gorgeous fabrics.

Vermont Star Party

By Brenda Clements Jones, 1994, Arlington, Virginia 29" x 45".

Brenda loves anything to do with the stars. The three-dimensional effect achieved by changing the angles of the Star blocks is well worth the challenge. Try making this quilt with lights, mediums, and darks in a single color family.

Materials: 44"-wide fabric

1 1/3 yds. dark fabric
2 1/3 yds. medium fabric
1 1/3 yds. light fabric
1 3/8 yds. backing
1/2 yd. for binding
33" x 49" piece of batting

Cutting

There are nine different blocks in this quilt. Each has 17 pieces. Each of the other 21 blocks is either a copy of one of the nine blocks or a mirror image of it. Use the pattern on the pullout at the back of the book to trace templates for the Star blocks. See "Making Templates" on pages 9–10. If your color placement is reversible, you can make the same block and turn it 180° for the mirror-image block. If the color varies from top to bottom or side to side in your blocks, use the templates in reverse for the mirror-image blocks. Refer to the chart on page 37 and the quilt photograph for color and block placement.

For each of the dark blocks in Rows 2, 4, and 6
From the dark fabrics, cut:
1 each of templates 1, 3, 5, 7, 11, 13, 15, and 17

From the medium fabrics, cut:
1 each of templates 2, 4, 6, 8 10, 12, 14, and 16

For the star center, cut:
1 template 9 for each block, from light, medium, or dark fabric. Change the value from block to block.

For each of the light blocks in Rows 1, 3, and 5
From the light fabrics, cut:
1 each of templates 1, 3, 5, 7, 11, 13, 15, and 17

From the medium fabrics, cut:
1 each of templates 2, 4, 6, 8, 10, 12, 14, and 16

For the star center, cut:
1 template 9 for each block, from light, medium, or dark fabric. Change the value from block to block.

Assembling the Blocks

All the blocks are Variable Stars skewed to various degrees and, regardless of their shape, are assembled in the same order. Be very careful, however, because the shapes are similar. *To help you orient these odd-shaped pieces, mark block letters and numbers in the seam allowances of each piece to identify the adjoining pieces.*

1. Arrange the pieces in 3 horizontal rows as shown. Sew the pieces together in rows.
2. Sew the rows together to complete each block, matching seam intersections carefully.

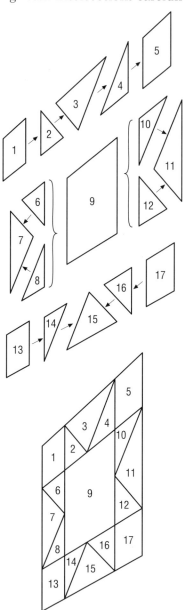

Assembling the Quilt

1. Arrange the blocks and sew them together into vertical rows as shown in the quilt plan. Press the seams in even-numbered rows in one direction; press the seams in odd-numbered rows in the opposite direction.
2. Sew the rows together, matching the seams carefully.

Finishing

1. Layer the quilt top with batting and backing. Baste the layers together.
2. Quilt as desired.
3. Bind with single-layer bias binding to make it easier to handle the angled edges of the quilt. See the note under "Binding your Quilt" on page 19.
4. Label your quilt.

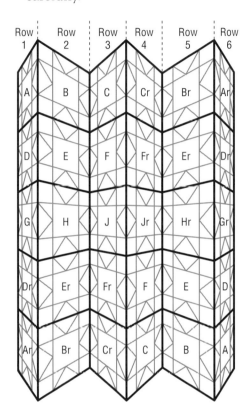

Row 1	Row 2	Row 3	Row 4	Row 5	Row 6
A	B	C	Cr	Br	Ar
D	E	F	Fr	Er	Dr
G	H	J	Jr	Hr	Gr
Dr	Er	Fr	F	E	D
Ar	Br	Cr	C	B	A

Stars Over the Mountains

By Kay Lettau, 1991, Annandale, Virginia, 88" x 105½".

This beautiful Feathered Star quilt was begun in 1991 in a class Kay taught with Judy Spahn at The Quilt Patch. Judy taught the drafting and Kay taught the machine piecing. Kay made one block in scraps of black, brown, and gray as a class sample. She always makes sample blocks to try to find the possible pitfalls. This one was so much fun she kept on sewing until she had enough for this exquisite quilt.

Materials: 44"-wide fabric

6³/₄ yds. total of assorted lights
²/₃ yd. total of assorted mediums
6⁵/₈ yds. total of assorted darks
1⁵/₈ yds. light stripe for lattice
3¹/₈ yds. dark for outer border
9¹/₄ yds. for backing
³/₄ yd. for binding
95" x 112" piece of batting

Making One 16" Feathered Star Block

When Kay made her Stars Over the Mountains quilt, she did not cut, or even select, all of her fabrics at once. She made a star and then cut another one. She used her leftover fabrics for subsequent stars and the pieced border.

The following instructions are for cutting and piecing one Feathered Star block at a time the way Kay did. Use 5 dark prints, 1 medium print, and 3 light prints for each block. The instructions for assembling the quilt top and making the pieced Delectable Mountains Border begin on page 41.

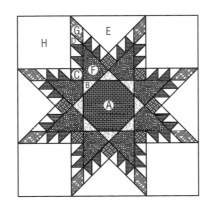

Cutting

Use the templates on pages 45–46.

From dark fabric #1, cut:
1 template A, for block center

From dark fabric #2, cut:
8 template C

From dark fabric #3, cut:
1 square, 10" x 10", for half–square triangle units

From dark fabric #4, cut:
8 template F, for star point centers

From dark fabric #5, cut:
8 template G for star point tips

From medium fabric, cut:
8 template B, for triangles surrounding center

From light fabric #1, cut:
4 template E, for background triangles

From light fabric #2, cut:
16 template D
1 square, 10" x 10", for half-square triangle units

From light fabric #3, cut:
4 template H, for background squares

Making Half-Square Triangle Units

To make half-square triangle units for one Feathered Star block, use two 10" squares, one from a dark fabric and one from a light fabric. You should get 32 half-square triangle units from each pair of 10" squares.

1. Layer the squares of fabric right sides together and cut 2"-wide bias strips from both fabrics at the same time.

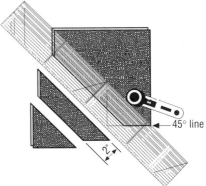

2. Sew the pairs of strips together on the long bias edges, using a ¹/₄"-wide seam allowance. Press the seams open. Place template C on the right side of a bias-strip unit, lining up opposite corners of the template with the seam line. Trace around the template. Start at one end and trace a string of squares the length of the seam line.

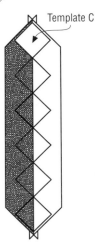

3. Carefully cut out the half-square triangle units just inside the drawn lines. You will have two odd-shaped pieces left over. Sew the long straight edges of these together, press, and cut another set of squares.

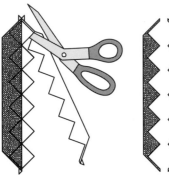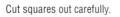

Cut squares out carefully. Leftover pieces Sew leftover pieces together, then trace and cut squares.

Piecing the Feathered Star

Before you begin to stitch your Feathered Star blocks, make sure you are sewing with an accurate and consistent 1/4"-wide seam allowance. Kay likes to use lightweight, all-cotton thread in a neutral color, and a short stitch length (15 to 18 stitches per inch).

1. Sew 4 of piece B to a piece A to form Unit 2. Press the seams toward A.

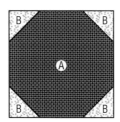

Unit 2

2. Sew together 2 template C half-square triangle units to form Unit 1, and 2 to form Unit 1a. Press the seams open carefully.

Unit 1
Make 8

Unit 1a
Make 8

3. Sew a piece D to each Unit 1. Sew a piece D and a piece C to each Unit 1a. Press the seams open.

Unit 1   Unit 1a

4. Add a Unit 1 to each piece E, sewing a partial seam from point X to point Y only. Press the seam toward E.

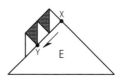

Make 4

5. Add Unit 1a, sewing a partial seam from point X to point Y only. Press the seam toward E.

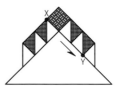

6. Add a piece F to each unit. Press the seam toward F.

7. Sew piece B to piece F. Press the seam toward F. Add this to each of the units. Press the seam toward B/F.

8. Sew piece G to piece D. Press the seam toward D. Add a G/D to each of the 4 remaining Units 1. Press the seam open.

Make 4

9. Add a piece H to each Unit 1. Press the seam toward H.

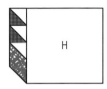

10. Sew remaining piece G to piece D. Press the seams toward D.
11. Sew a piece C and a G/D to each of the 4 remaining Units 1a. Press the C seam toward C and the G/D seam open.

Make 4

12. Add Unit 1a to the top of piece H as shown. Press the seam toward H.

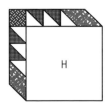

Make 4

13. Arrange the pieced units in rows as shown. Sew the units together, pinning carefully to match the points. As you stitch the H and E Units together in Rows 1 and 3, sew from the inner corner outward. Then finish stitching

the partial seams from points Y to the edge of the block. Sew the rows together in the same manner.

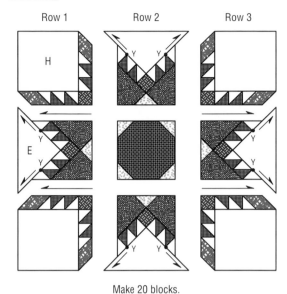

Make 20 blocks.

Assembling the Quilt Top

Making the Four-Patch Cornerstones and Lattice

Cutting

From the light stripe, cut:
17 strips, each 2" x 54" from the lengthwise grain of the fabric; crosscut into 49 lattice strips, each 2" x 16½"

From the assorted light fabrics, cut:
3 squares, each 10" x 10"

From the assorted dark fabrics, cut:
3 squares, each 10" x 10"
30 Template I

1. Using 10" squares of the light and dark fabrics, cut 1½"-wide bias strips. Make 90 half-square triangle units using template I. Refer to "Making Half-Square Triangle Units" on pages 39–40.
2. Sew 2 half-square triangle units together. Press the seams open.
3. Sew 1 half-square triangle unit to a piece I. Press the seams open.

4. Sew the two units together. Press the seams open. Make 30 cornerstones.

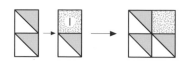

5. To make pieced lattice strips, join four 2" x 16½" light-striped rectangles and 5 cornerstones as shown.

Make 6

6. Using 4 Feathered Star blocks and 5 plain lattice strips for each row, construct 5 rows of blocks as shown.

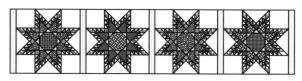

Make 5

7. Sew the rows of blocks and the lattice rows together as shown in the quilt plan on page 44.

Cutting Borders

From the assorted light fabrics, cut:
10 squares, each 10" x 10"
36 Template M

From the assorted dark fabrics, cut:
10 squares, each 10" x 10"
40 Template K
40 Template L
2 squares, each 6⅞" x 6⅞"; cut once diagonally for a total of 4 triangles for piece N (outer corners)

From the dark fabric for the outer border, cut:
2 strips, each 3½" x 90"
2 strips, each 3½" x 108"

Piecing the Delectable Mountains Border

1. Using 10" squares of assorted dark and light fabrics, cut 1½"-wide bias strips, following directions for "Making Half-Square Triangle Units" on pages 39–40. Cut 360 half-square triangle units using template J as a cutting guide.
2. Sew 4 half-square triangle units together. Press the seams open.

Make 80

3. Sew a half-square triangle strip to each piece K. Press the seam toward K.

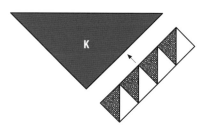

4. Add a triangle L and another half-square triangle unit to the remaining 40 strip units, as shown. Press the seams open.

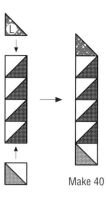

Make 40

5. Sew a half-square triangle strip to the other short side of each piece K. Press seams toward K.

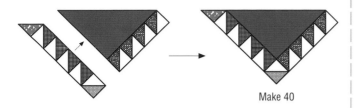

Make 40

6. Construct 2 border strips, using 9 triangle units and 8 piece M in each. Press the seams toward piece M.

7. Sew the border strips to the top and bottom of the quilt, beginning and ending your stitching ¹/4" from the ends.
8. Construct 2 side border strips; use 11 triangle units and 10 piece M in each. Press seams toward piece M.
9. Pin the border strips to the sides of the quilt, matching the point of the center triangle unit with the middle of the center lattice strip. Pin the end triangle units so that the center of the unit is slightly less than ¹/2" from the corner.

Center of triangle unit is approximately ¹/2" from corner.

Stop stitching ¹/4" from corner.

10. Sew the border strips to the sides of the quilt, beginning and ending your stitching ¹/4" from the corners.
11. Referring to "Borders with Mitered Corners" on page 16, miter the corners of the Delectable Mountains border and trim the seam allowance to ¹/4". Add a triangle N to each corner of the quilt.

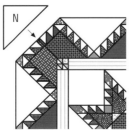

N

Adding the Outer Border

1. Referring to "Borders with Mitered Corners" on page 16, measure, trim, and sew the strips of dark border fabric to the quilt.
2. Miter the corners of the border and trim the seam allowances to ¹/4".

Finishing

1. Layer the quilt with batting and backing. Baste the layers together.
2. Quilt as desired.
3. Bind the edges and enjoy your masterpiece, and don't forget a label!

Quilt Patch Recipe
My Boursin
By Leslie Pfeifer

After living in Europe for eight years, I came to love the French herb cheeses, and Boursin in particular. It was costly enough in Europe, but in the States it was really more than I could justify, especially since I could eat so much of it. Here is my own version, in a slightly reduced-fat format. It's a standard at our annual holiday party.

2 to 4 fresh garlic cloves, depending on size and love of garlic
Two 8-ounce packages regular or light cream cheese at room temperature (I use one package of each.)
8 ounces butter or butter substitute (at room temperature)
¹/3 teaspoon freshly ground pepper
¹/2 teaspoon each of thyme, basil, oregano, dill, and marjoram
Salt, if desired (I never add salt.)

Mince garlic in food processor. Add remaining ingredients and process until blended, soft, and creamy. Refrigerate overnight or freeze. I often make it several days ahead. Once made, it keeps a long time, given a chance.

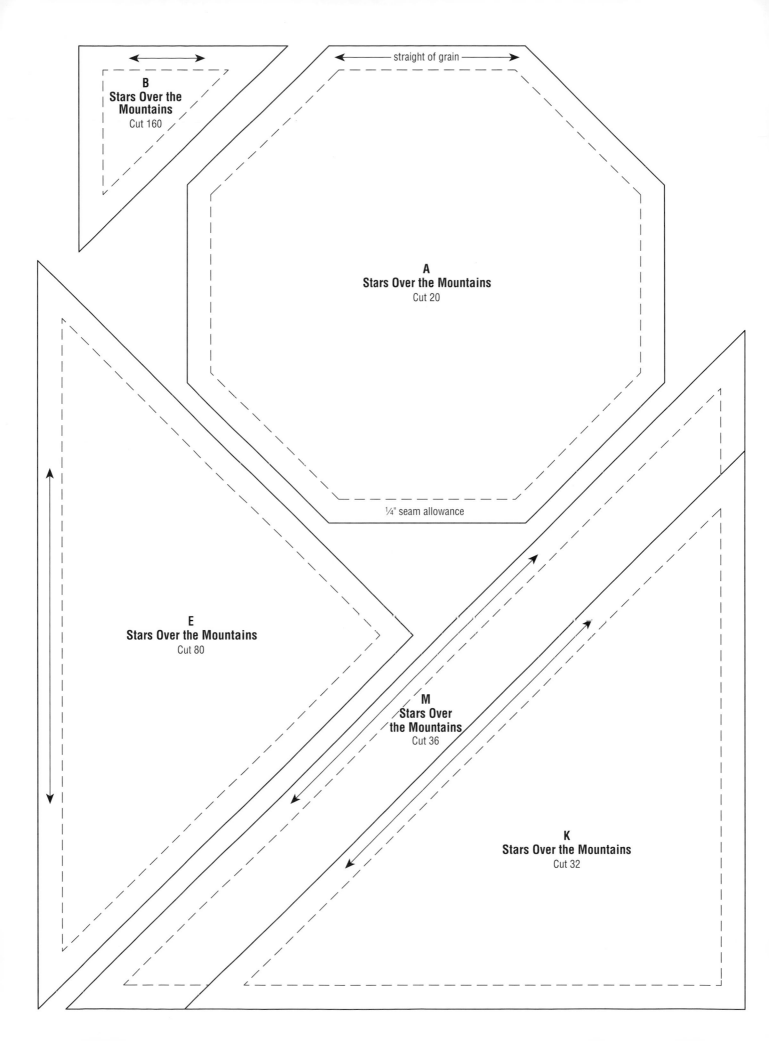

B
Stars Over the Mountains
Cut 160

straight of grain

A
Stars Over the Mountains
Cut 20

¼" seam allowance

E
Stars Over the Mountains
Cut 80

M
Stars Over the Mountains
Cut 36

K
Stars Over the Mountains
Cut 32

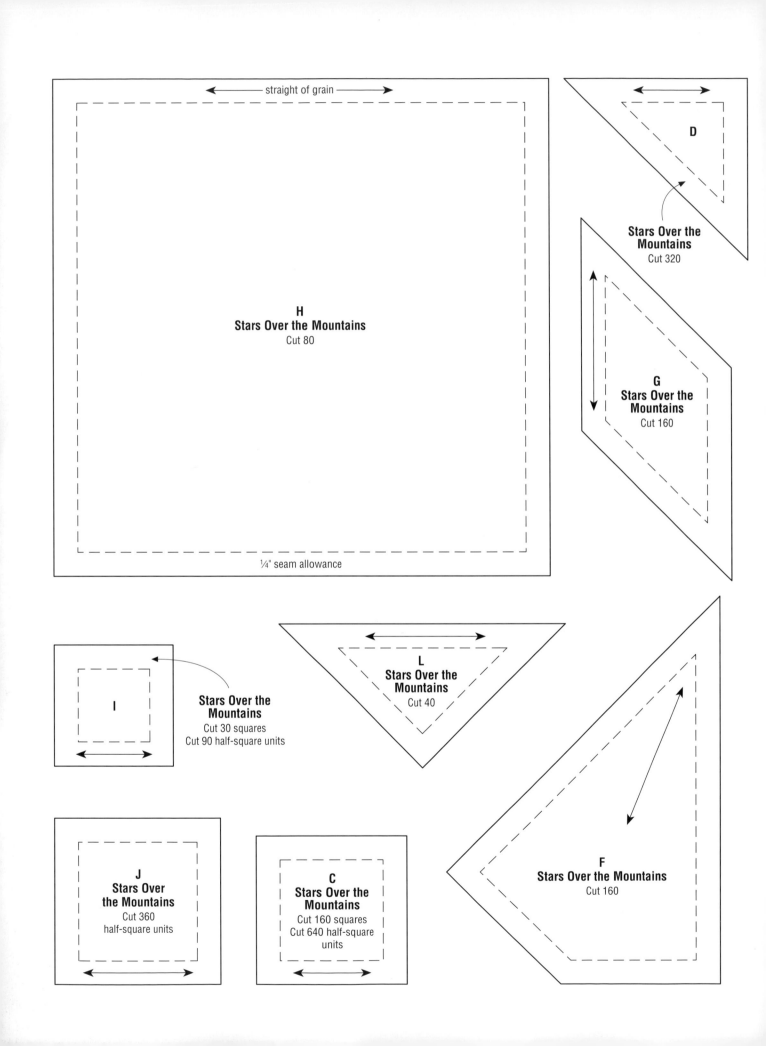

straight of grain

H
Stars Over the Mountains
Cut 80

¼" seam allowance

D

Stars Over the Mountains
Cut 320

G
Stars Over the Mountains
Cut 160

I

Stars Over the Mountains
Cut 30 squares
Cut 90 half-square units

L
Stars Over the Mountains
Cut 40

J
Stars Over the Mountains
Cut 360
half-square units

C
Stars Over the Mountains
Cut 160 squares
Cut 640 half-square units

F
Stars Over the Mountains
Cut 160

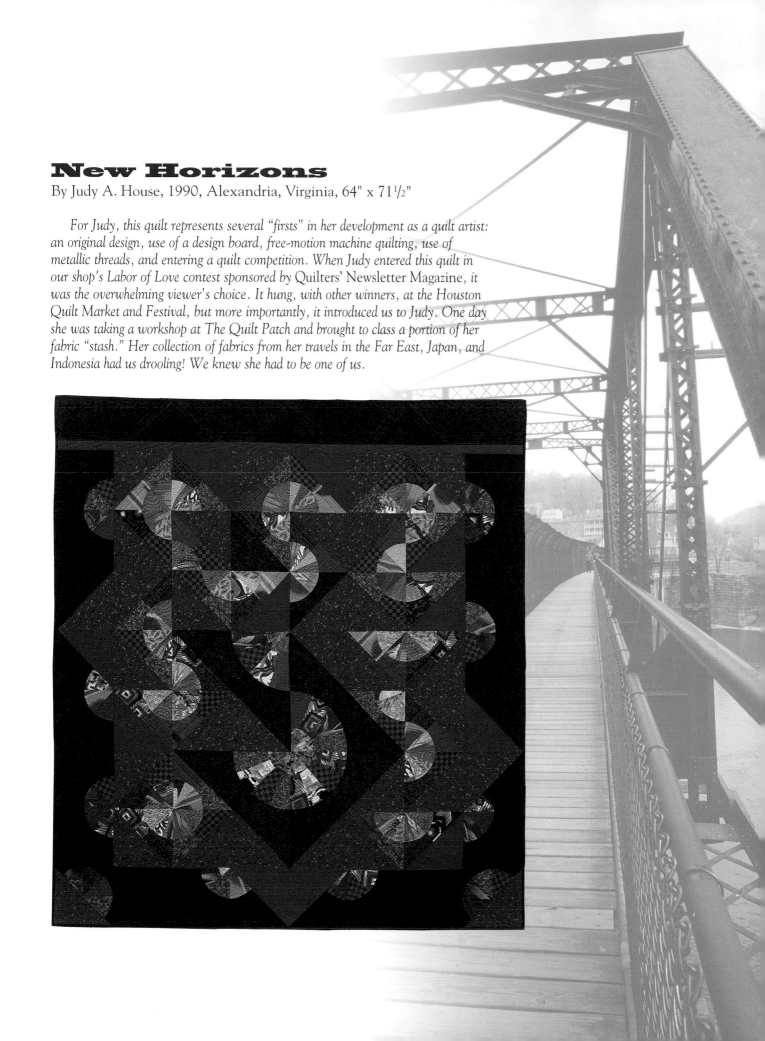

New Horizons

By Judy A. House, 1990, Alexandria, Virginia, 64" x 71½"

For Judy, this quilt represents several "firsts" in her development as a quilt artist: an original design, use of a design board, free-motion machine quilting, use of metallic threads, and entering a quilt competition. When Judy entered this quilt in our shop's Labor of Love contest sponsored by Quilters' Newsletter Magazine, *it was the overwhelming viewer's choice. It hung, with other winners, at the Houston Quilt Market and Festival, but more importantly, it introduced us to Judy. One day she was taking a workshop at The Quilt Patch and brought to class a portion of her fabric "stash." Her collection of fabrics from her travels in the Far East, Japan, and Indonesia had us drooling! We knew she had to be one of us.*

Materials: 44"-wide fabric

The Quilt Patch features fabric "tidbits," pieces measuring 9" x 22", or a "fat-eighth" of a yard. Judy suggests using tidbits of many different fabrics to achieve the wonderfully complex look of this quilt.

1$\frac{1}{8}$ yds. red focus print
$\frac{5}{8}$ yd. red accent print
$\frac{2}{3}$ yd. black print #1
1 yd. black print #2
1 yd. black print #3
$\frac{1}{4}$ yd. purple print for top border
2$\frac{1}{4}$ yds. total of assorted dark purple and teal prints (18 tidbits)
1 yd. total of assorted light lavender and teal prints (8 tidbits)
$\frac{3}{8}$ yd. total of assorted light lavender prints (3 tidbits)
$\frac{5}{8}$ yd. total of assorted dark purple prints (5 tidbits)
6" x 8" piece of dark gray
2$\frac{1}{2}$ yds. for backing
$\frac{3}{4}$ yd. for binding
70" x 78" piece of batting

Quilt Patch Pointer

Judy machine quilted "New Horizons" with metallic threads. Here are some of her pointers for using these special threads:

❖❖ Clean your machine before beginning.
❖❖ Use a good quality thread. You can use metallic on the top and rayon or cotton thread in the bobbin.
❖❖ Use a needle designed for metallic threads, such as a #90 topstitch needle.
❖❖ Slightly loosen the top tension on your machine.
❖❖ Do not thread the last thread guide just above the needle.
❖❖ If you do free-motion quilting, be sure to lift the presser foot prior to threading the machine.
❖❖ Most important when you use specialty threads—slow down and develop a rhythm. Relax.

Cutting

Use the templates on the pullout pattern at the back of the book.

From the red focus print, cut:
4 strips, each 8$\frac{7}{8}$" x 42"; crosscut into 16 squares, each 8$\frac{7}{8}$" x 8$\frac{7}{8}$". Cut each square in half diagonally for a total of 32 half-square triangles for piece L. You will use 31.

From the red accent print, cut:
2 strips, each 8$\frac{7}{8}$" x 42"; crosscut into 6 squares, each 8$\frac{7}{8}$" x 8$\frac{7}{8}$". Cut each square once diagonally into a total of 12 half-square triangles for piece L. You will use 11.

From black #1, cut:
2 strips, each 8$\frac{1}{2}$" x 24$\frac{1}{2}$"
2 strips, each 6$\frac{1}{2}$" x 16$\frac{1}{2}$"
1 square, 6$\frac{7}{8}$" x 6$\frac{7}{8}$"; cut once diagonally for piece I.
1 each of templates 7 and 7r

From black #2, cut:
2 strips, each 8$\frac{1}{2}$" x 24$\frac{1}{2}$"
1 strip, 6$\frac{1}{2}$" x 16$\frac{1}{2}$"
1 square, 6$\frac{7}{8}$" x 6$\frac{7}{8}$"; cut once diagonally for piece I.
2 template 7
1 template 7r
1 template 2

From black #3, cut:
2 strips, each 8$\frac{1}{2}$" x 40$\frac{1}{2}$"
1 strip, 6$\frac{1}{2}$" x 16$\frac{1}{2}$"
1 square, 8$\frac{7}{8}$" x 8$\frac{7}{8}$"; cut once diagonally for piece L.
1 square, 6$\frac{7}{8}$" x 6$\frac{7}{8}$"; cut once diagonally for piece I.
1 template 7
2 template 7r
1 template 2r

From the purple print for top border, cut:
2 strips, each 2" x 32$\frac{1}{4}$"

From the assorted dark purples and teals, cut:
32 template 2
32 template 2r
36 template 3

From the assorted light lavenders and teals, cut:
43 template 3

From the assorted light lavenders, cut:
40 template 4

From the assorted dark purples, cut:
8 template 5
14 template 6

From the dark gray, cut:
2 template 6
2 template 3

Assembling the Blocks

Blocks A, B, G, and H

(See quilt layout on page 50.)

Refer to the illustration below to determine the fabric placement for the large triangle in each block. Color placement for the other block pieces is up to you.

Block A
Red Focus
Make 11

Block B
Red Accent
Make 3

Block G
Black #3
Make 1

Block H
Red Focus
Make 1

1. Sew together 2 of piece 3.
2. Sew piece 2 to piece 2r. Pin and sew the two units together along the curve, carefully matching the center seams.
3. Sew a large triangle L of the required color to the unit.

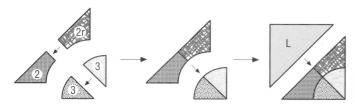

Blocks C and E

Construct these blocks in the same manner as Block A. Refer to the illustration for fabric placement of large triangle L.

Block C
Red Accent
Make 2

Block E
Red Focus
Make 3

1. Sew together 4 of piece 4.
2. Follow steps 2–3 below left to complete the block.

Blocks D and F

Construct these blocks in the same manner as A and C.

Block D
Red Accent
Make 2

Block F
Red Focus
Make 7

1. Sew together 2 of piece 4 and a piece 3 as shown.
2. Complete the block, following steps 2–3 for Block A at left.

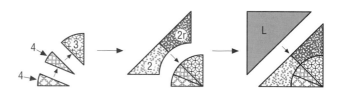

Block I

Construct this block in the same manner as Block A, but do not add a large triangle.

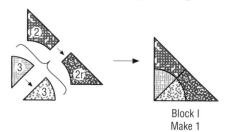

Block I
Make 1

Block J

Construct this block in the same manner as Block F, but do not add a large triangle.

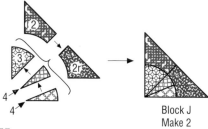

Block J
Make 2

Block K

1. Sew 2 of piece 6 together. Add piece 5 along the small curve.

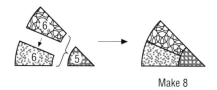

Make 8

2. Sew the 2 units from step 1 together.
3. Sew piece 7 to piece 7r.
4. Pin and sew the units together along the curve, carefully matching the center seams.

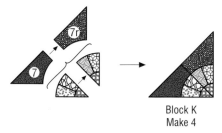

Block K
Make 4

Assembling the Quilt

Referring to the quilt layout above right, arrange the blocks into rows as shown and sew them together. Press the seams in even-numbered

rows in one direction and the seams in odd-numbered rows in the opposite direction. Sew the rows together, matching the seams between the blocks.

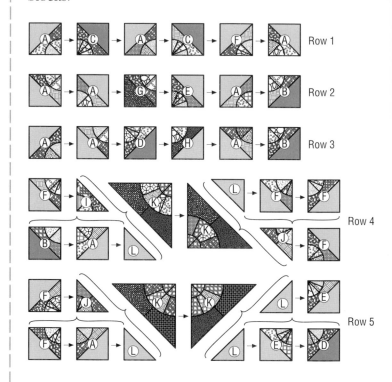

Row 1
Row 2
Row 3
Row 4
Row 5

Adding the Borders

1. Sew together 4 of the dark purple and teal piece 3 to make half-circles. Turn under the 1/4"-wide seam allowance on the curve and baste.
2. Sew together 3 of the dark purple and teal piece 3 to make partial circles. Turn under the 1/4"-wide seam allowance on the curve and baste.

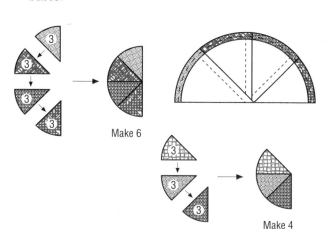

Make 6

Make 4

Bottom Border

1. Trim the right end of an $8^1/_2$" x $24^1/_2$" strip of black #1 at a 45° angle. Appliqué a partial circle, then sew a red accent-print triangle to the trimmed end as shown.

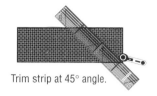

Trim strip at 45° angle.

Add half-circle and triangle.

2. Trim the left end of an $8^1/_2$" x $24^1/_2$" strip of black #2 at a 45° angle. Appliqué a partial circle, then add a red accent-print triangle as shown.

3. Sew the two strips together at the triangles and add the strip to the bottom of the quilt.

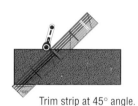

Trim strip at 45° angle.

Add half-circle and triangle.

Bottom Border

Left Border

1. Trim the right end of the $8^1/_2$" x $24^1/_2$" strip of black #2 at a 45° angle. Sew a red focus-print triangle to the trimmed end.

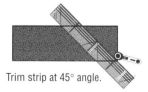

Trim strip at 45° angle.

Add triangle

2. Trim both ends of an $8^1/_2$" x $40^1/_2$" strip of black #3 at a 45° angle. To the right end, appliqué a half circle, then add a red focus-print triangle. To the left end, add a partial circle and a red accent-print triangle.

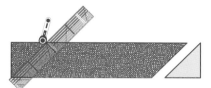

3. Join the two border strips as shown.

Left Border

4. Place the left border strip along the side of the quilt top, matching the seam of the border to the row seam on the quilt top as indicated by the arrow. In the border seam allowance, mark the top and bottom row seams for placement of 2 half circles.

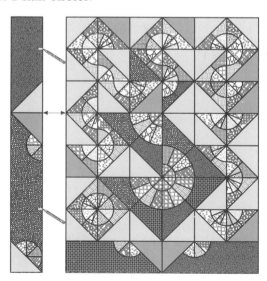

5. Appliqué 2 half-circles in place on the border strip, matching their centers to the marks in the border seam allowance.

6. Sew the border to the left side of the quilt.

Right Border

1. Trim the right end of the $8\frac{1}{2}$" x $24\frac{1}{2}$" strip of black #1 at a 45° angle. Appliqué a partial circle, then add a red focus-print triangle.
2. Trim the left end of the same strip at a 45° angle. Appliqué a half-circle, then add a red focus-print triangle to that end.

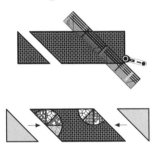

3. Trim the left end of the $8\frac{1}{2}$" x $40\frac{1}{2}$" strip of black #3 at a 45° angle. Add a red accent-print triangle.

4. Sew the strips together at the triangles.

Right Border

5. Lay the strip along the right side of the quilt top, as with the left border. In the seam allowance of the border strip, mark the row seams as shown for placement of the remaining 2 half-circles.

6. Appliqué the half-circles to the right border and sew the border strip to the quilt top.

Top Border

1. Trim the $6\frac{1}{2}$" x $16\frac{1}{2}$" black strips at a 45° angle and sew the black triangles (piece I) to the trimmed ends as shown.

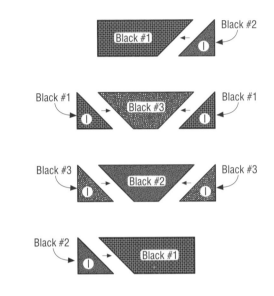

2. Arrange the sections and sew them together as shown.
3. Sew the 2"-wide purple strips end to end to make one long strip. Sew the pieced strip to the bottom edge of the border. Sew the border to the top edge of the quilt.

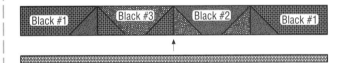

Finishing

Judy likes to create interesting backs on her quilts, so she pieces the leftovers into the backing. As with most of Judy's quilts, there are no rules, so you can add pieced units, strips, and leftover hunks of fabric to the back. Anything goes!

1. Layer the top with batting and backing.
2. Quilt as desired.
3. Bind and label your New Horizons quilt.

Stellafane '90
(or The One That Got Away)

By Brenda Clements Jones, 1990,
Arlington, Virginia, 45" x 55".

    *This quilt was inspired by Stellafane 1990, an amateur telescope makers'
convention held every summer in Springfield, Vermont. One evening, while many
telescopes were focused on deep-sky objects, a dim aurora was observed to the
north. Brenda believed it was about to be obscured by clouds, and, faced with a ten-
hour drive home the next day, she decided to turn in. The next morning, everyone
in her astronomy club raved about that aurora. The sky had glowed with the
Northern Lights. Flames leaped from the treetops and colors changed with every
moment. Brenda had missed it all! There is no instant replay in nature, so Brenda
had to create her own aurora of five-pointed stars, scattered across a night of dark
rainbow colors, with a stream of light slashing through the middle.*

Materials: 44"-wide fabric

This scrap quilt contains myriad colors. A red value finder like the Ruby Beholder™ (produced by That Patchwork Place) is an invaluable aid in choosing fabrics for this quilt because the design requires changing color values along the "beam of light."

Use print fabrics in each of the colors listed below. You need the yardage given for *each* shade listed for *each* of the colors.

Red-purple, green, and orange
$1/8$ yd. very light
$1/8$ yd. medium light
$1/4$ yd. medium dark
$1/3$ yd. deep dark

Purple and yellow-gold
$1/8$ yd. very light
$1/4$ yd. medium light
$1/4$ yd. medium dark
$1/3$ yd. deep dark

Blue and red
$1/8$ yd. very light
$1/8$ yd. medium light
$1/3$ yd. medium dark
$1/2$ yd. deep dark

Gray
$1/4$ yd. or a fat eighth

Black
$2 1/4$ yds. for borders and binding

$3 1/2$ yds. for backing
49" x 59" piece of batting

Cutting and Assembling the Star Blocks

Brenda suggests that you cut and sew the blocks one at a time, following the instructions for each block, the placement chart, and the photograph on page 53. A design wall or layout surface is useful for getting the color placement correct. Label each Star block as you complete it.

1. Make plastic templates for each piece of Block B and Block E on page 59. (See "Making Templates" on pages 9–10.) Be sure to mark each template with the appropriate letter and number and trace the grain-line arrow on each one.
2. Notice that Block E also contains the template shapes for Blocks A, C, and D. To make Templates A3, A4, A5, and A6, trace the shaded areas of Block E as shown, ignoring the unnecessary interior lines.

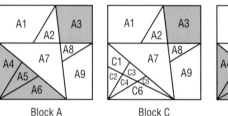
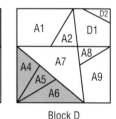

Block E

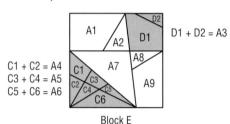

Block A   Block C   Block D

3. Cut the required pieces for each block, referring to the block directions the "Block Layout Chart" on page 58, and the color photo on page 53. *If you plan to hand piece this quilt, place the templates right-side down on the wrong side of the fabric for cutting and sewing.* Mark the seam intersections on the wrong side of each piece for accurate piecing.
4. Arrange the pieces for each block and assemble them as shown in the piecing diagrams that follow the cutting directions for each one.

Block A

Make the following number of A blocks in each color:
  5 red-purple
  4 purple
  9 blue
  5 green
  4 yellow-gold
  5 orange
  9 red

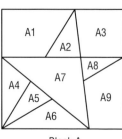

Block A

From the deep dark prints of each color, cut 1 each of the following pieces for each A block: A1, A3, A4, A6, and A9

From the medium dark prints of each color, cut 1 each of the following pieces for each A block: A2, A5, A7, and A8. Assemble as shown.

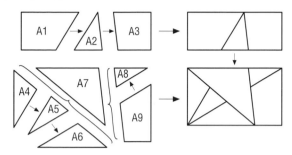

Block B

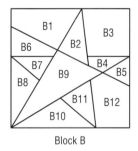

Block B

All of the B blocks fall within the "beam of light" that shines across the quilt, so pay particular attention to color placement. Refer to the chart on page 58 and to the photo on page 53.

For B Blocks, positions F2, H3, J4, L5, and N6:
Make 1 B block in each color: red-purple, blue, green, orange, and red.
1. From the deep dark prints of each color, cut 1 each of templates B1, B3, and B5.
2. From the medium dark prints of each color, cut 1 each of templates B2 and B4.
3. From the medium light prints of each color, cut 1 each of templates B6, B8, B10, and B12.
4. From the very light prints of each color, cut 1 each of templates B7, B9, and B11.

For B Blocks, positions F3, H4, J5, L6, and N7:
Make 1 B block in each color: red-purple, blue, green, orange, and red.

1. From the deep dark fabrics of each color, cut 1 each of template B6, B8, B10, and B12.
2. From the medium dark fabrics of each color, cut 1 each of templates B7, B9, and B11.
3. From the medium light fabrics of each color, cut 1 each of templates B1, B3, and B5.
4. From the very light fabrics of each color, cut 1 each of templates B2 and B4.
5. Arrange the pieces for each B block and, referring to the chart and the quilt photo, assemble them as shown.

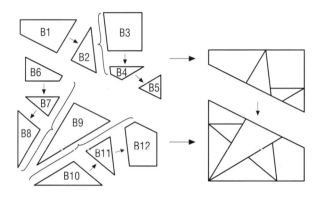

Block C

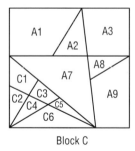

Block C

Make 1 C block in each color: purple, blue, yellow-gold, and red.
1. From the deep dark fabric of each color, cut 1 each of templates A1, A3, A9, C1, and C5.
2. From the medium dark fabric of each color, cut 1 each of templates A2, A7, A8, and C3.
3. From the medium light fabric of each color, cut 1 each of templates C2 and C6.
4. From the very light fabric of each color, cut 1 of template C4.

5. Referring to the chart on page 58 and the quilt photo on page 53, arrange the pieces for each C block and assemble as shown.

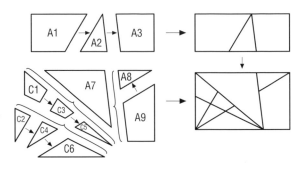

Block D

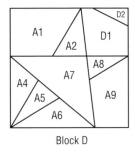

Block D

Make 1 D block in each color: purple, blue, yellow-gold, and red.
1. From the deep dark fabric of each color, cut 1 each of templates D1, A1, A4, A6, and A9.
2. From the medium dark fabric of each color, cut 1 each of templates A2, A5, A7, and A8.
3. From the medium light fabric of each color, cut 1 of template D2.
4. Referring to the chart on page 58 and the quilt photo on page 53, arrange the pieces for the D blocks and assemble as shown.

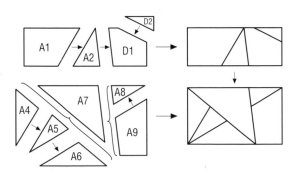

Block E

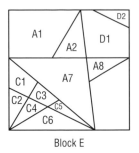

Block E

Make 1 E block in each color: purple, blue, yellow/gold, and red.
1. From the deep dark fabrics of each color, cut 1 each of template D2, C2, and C6.
2. From the medium dark fabrics of each color, cut 1 of template C4.
3. From the medium light fabrics of each color, cut 1 each of templates A1, A9, C1, C5, and D1.
4. From the very light fabrics of each color, cut 1 each of templates A2, A7, A8, and C3.
5. Referring to the chart on page 58 and the quilt photo on page 53, arrange the pieces for the E blocks and assemble as shown.

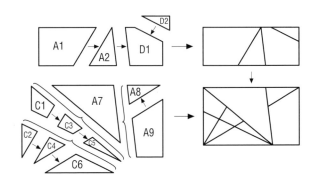

Assembling the Quilt Top

1. Place all the A blocks in groups by color. Sort all the B blocks by color, and so on.
2. Arrange the Star blocks in rows by color, being careful to turn each star to the position shown in the block layout chart. Not all stars face the same direction. There are two rows each of blue stars and red stars, and one row of each of the other colors.

3. Sew the blocks together into horizontal rows. Press the seams of the even-numbered rows in one direction and the seams in the odd-numbered rows in the opposite direction.
4. Sew the rows together, carefully matching the seams.

Adding the Border

1. From the black border fabric, cut 2 strips, each 5$\frac{1}{2}$" x 58", for the top and bottom borders. Cut 2 strips, each 5$\frac{1}{2}$" x 48", for the side borders.
2. From the gray fabric, cut 2 of template E (page 60). On the wrong side of each piece, mark the seam lines on both of the long edges.
3. Referring to "Borders with Mitered Corners" on page 16, add the 5$\frac{1}{2}$" x 58" black border strips to the top and bottom of the quilt top.
4. Center the 5$\frac{1}{2}$" x 48" black border strip along the left side of the quilt. With a marking pencil, lightly mark the lines where the "beam of light" crosses the border.

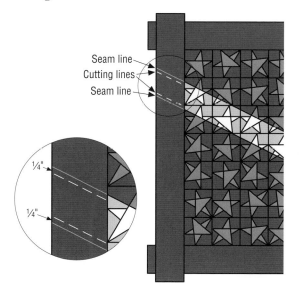

Seam line
Cutting lines
Seam line
1/4"
1/4"

5. Place the gray piece E on the black border, right sides together, lining up piece E with the upper cutting line on the border. Pin the pieces together and sew 1/4" from the edge of piece E. Cut the black border piece along the edge of piece E.

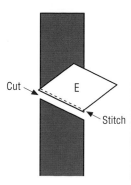

Cut
E
Stitch

6. Place the lower edge of piece E on the lower cutting line, right sides together. Matching the seam lines, pin the two together and sew 1/4" from the edge of piece E.

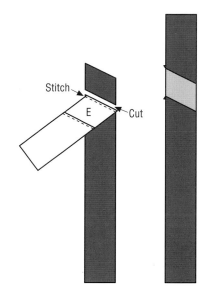

Stitch
E
Cut

7. Sew the side border to the left side of the quilt, carefully lining up the "beam of light" with the gray border piece.
8. Following steps 4–7 above, piece the gray beam of light into the right side border and add it to the quilt top.
9. Miter the border corners.

Finishing the Quilt

1. Layer the quilt with batting and backing. Baste the layers together.
2. Quilt as desired. Brenda quilted various sizes of concentric circles in the body of the quilt and scattered five-pointed stars, like those on pages 58 and 60, in the border.
3. Bind the edge with black binding.
4. Label your quilt.

Block Layout Chart

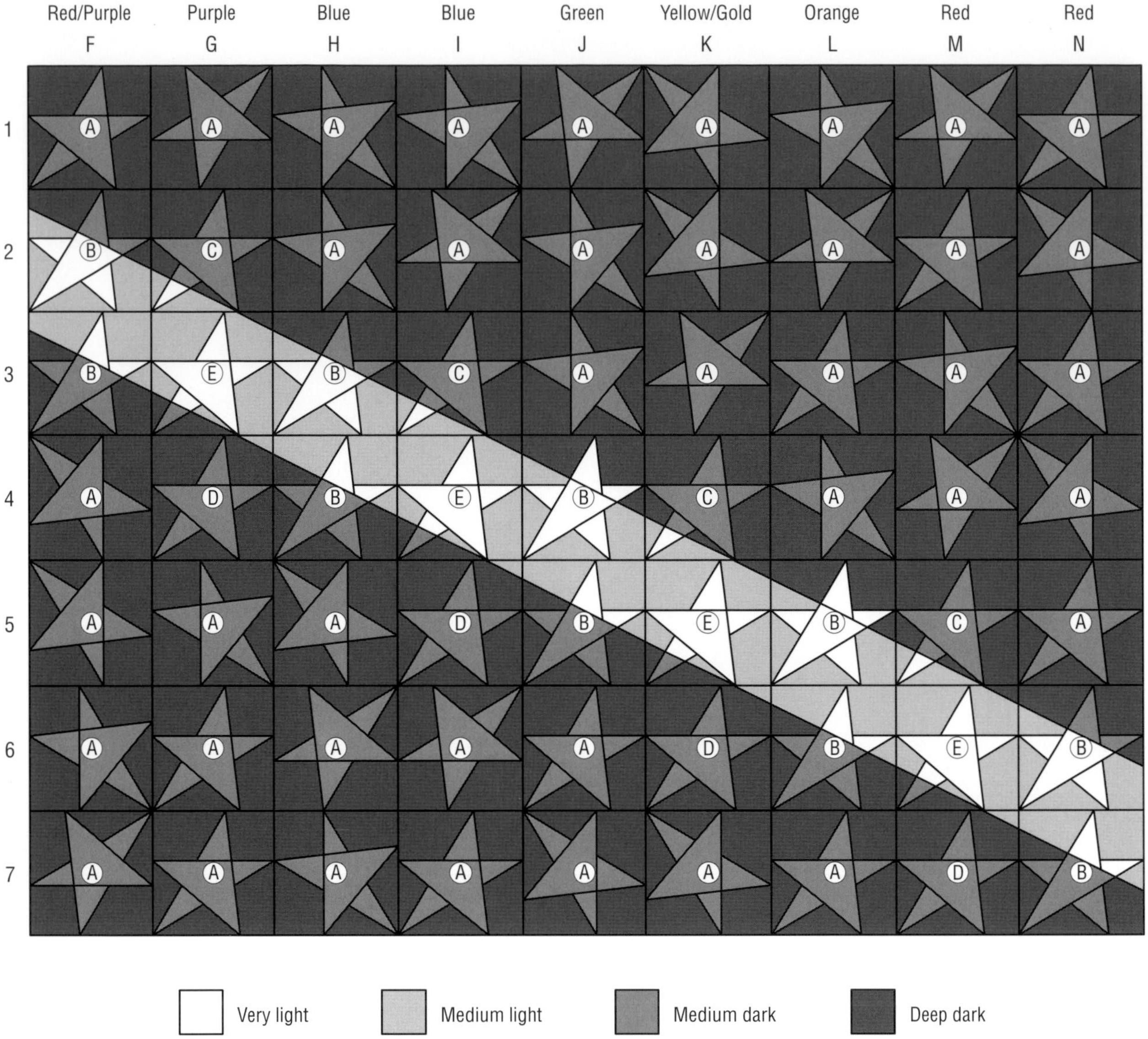

	Red/Purple F	Purple G	Blue H	Blue I	Green J	Yellow/Gold K	Orange L	Red M	Red N
1	A	A	A	A	A	A	A	A	A
2	B	C	A	A	A	A	A	A	A
3	B	E	B	C	A	A	A	A	A
4	A	D	B	E	B	C	A	A	A
5	A	A	A	D	B	E	B	C	A
6	A	A	A	A	A	D	B	E	B
7	A	A	A	A	A	A	A	D	B

Legend:
- Very light
- Medium light
- Medium dark
- Deep dark

Quilting Patterns

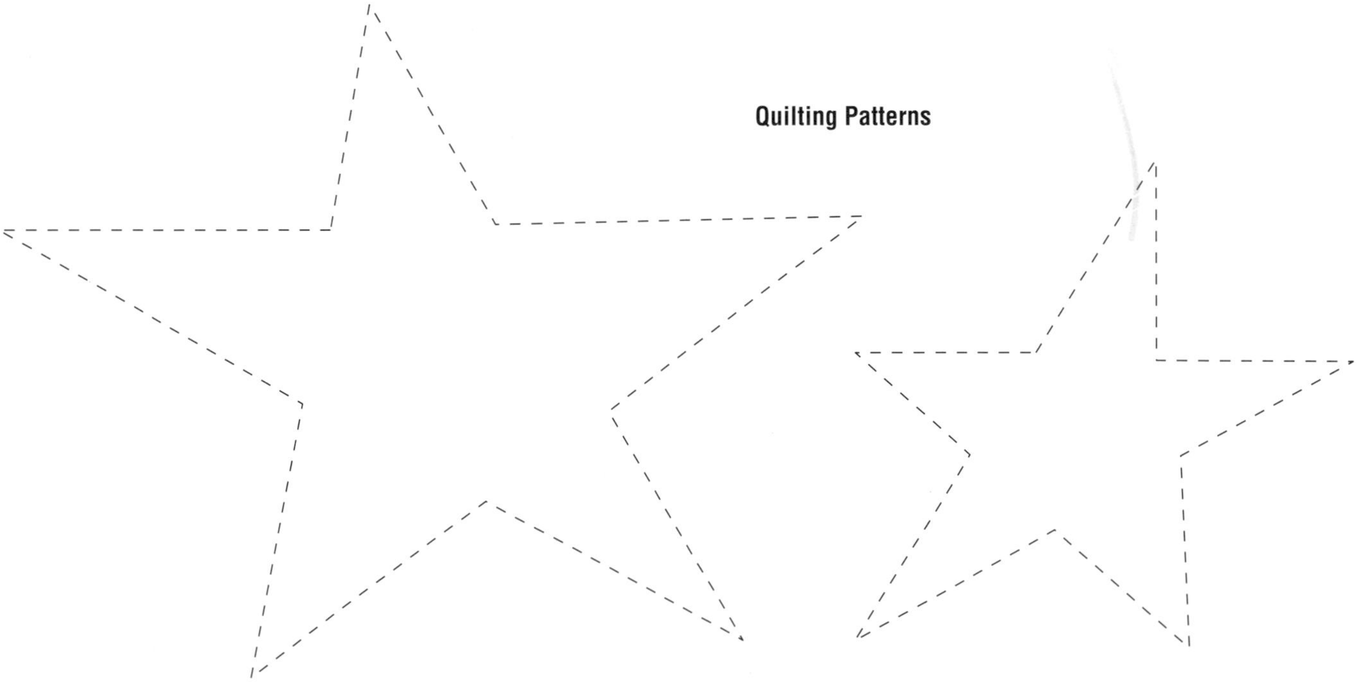

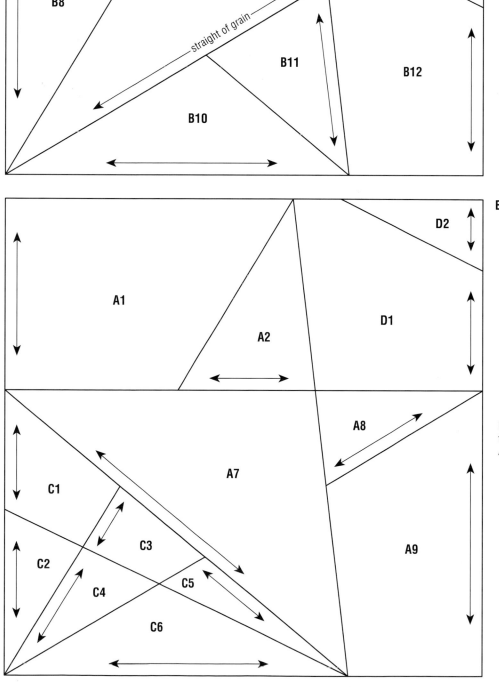

Block B

B1

B3

B2

B6

B7

B4

B5

B9

B8

straight of grain

B11

B12

B10

Block E

D2

A1

D1

A2

A8

C1

A7

C3

C2

A9

C4

C5

C6

Blocks A, C, and D require templates
from Block E. To make Templates A3,
A4, A5 and A6, see step 2 on page 54.

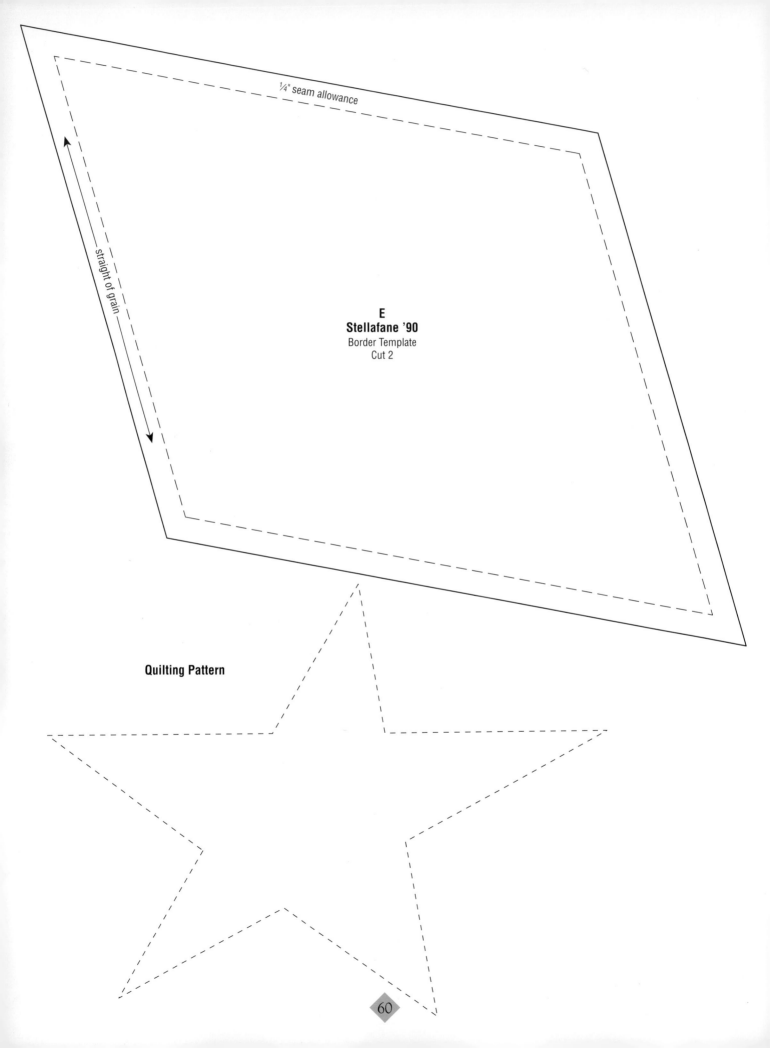

¼" seam allowance

straight of grain

E
Stellafane '90
Border Template
Cut 2

Quilting Pattern

Riot of Roses

By Brenda Clements Jones, 1992, Arlington, Virginia, 60" x 72".

Brenda's Mariner's Compass, a scrap quilt in a variety of colors, is dominated by purples. She set the blocks on point with alternating blocks of tan. The border is a series of partial compasses. Brenda made it for her cousin, Judith, who lives in Revere, Pennsylvania. Judith wishes we would stop borrowing it for shows and photographing; she wants it to stay home for awhile! We can't blame her, so special thanks to Judith for letting us include it in this book.

Brenda used a different background for each compass, and every compass uses different fabrics. We have provided the total amount of each fabric you need, but using scraps is certainly encouraged.

Materials: 44"-wide fabric

3¹/₃ yds. total of light background prints
⁷/₈ yd. total of medium fabrics for star points
¹/₂ yd. total of medium dark fabrics for star points
²/₃ yd. total of dark fabrics for star points
¹/₄ yd. total for centers
1³/₄ yds. for alternate blocks
¹/₂ yd. for inner border
1¹/₂ yds. for outer border
4¹/₂ yds. backing
³/₄ yd. for binding
67" x 80" piece of batting

Cutting for the Mariner's Compass Blocks

Use Riot of Roses templates on the pullout patterns at the back of the book. If you use a different background fabric for each compass, be sure to cut 16 template A to match the background square for each block.

From the light background fabrics, cut:
320 template A (16 for each)
20 squares, each 9¹/₂" x 9¹/₂"

From the medium fabrics, cut:
160 template B (8 for each)

From the medium dark fabrics, cut;
80 template C (4 for each)

From the dark fabric, cut:
80 template D (4 for each)

From the center fabrics, cut:
20 template E (1 for each)

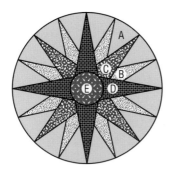

Mariner's Compass

Cutting for Alternate Blocks and Setting Triangles

From the alternate-block fabric, cut:
3 strips, each 9¹/₂" x 42"; crosscut into 12 squares, each 9¹/₂" x 9¹/₂".
2 strips, each 14" x 42"; crosscut into 4 squares, each 14" x 14". Cut each square twice diagonally for a total of 16 triangles. You will use 14 for side setting triangles.
2 squares, each 7¹/₄" x 7¹/₄"; cut each square once diagonally for a total of 4 triangles for the corners of the quilt.

Cutting for Borders

From the inner border fabric, cut:
7 strips, each 1¹/₂" x 42"

From the outer border fabric, cut:
8 strips, each 5¹/₂" x 42"

Cutting for Border Compasses

From the light background fabrics, cut:
132 template A (12 each for the corner compasses and 6 each for the half-compasses)
28 template BA

From the medium fabrics, cut:
52 template B (6 each for the corner compasses and 2 each for the half-compasses)
14 template BB
14 template BB reversed

From the medium dark fabrics, cut:
26 template C (3 each for the corner compasses and 1 each for the half-compasses)
8 template CD
8 template CD reversed

From the dark fabrics, cut:
4 template D
14 template BD
14 template BD reversed

From the center fabrics, cut:
4 template E

Mariner's Compass Block Assembly

To make each Mariner's Compass block:

1. Sew 2 of piece A to piece B to make Unit 1.

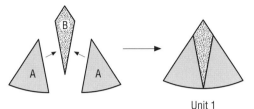

Unit 1
Make 8

2. Sew 2 of Unit 1 to piece C.

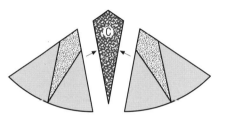

3. Add a piece D to make Unit 2.

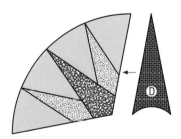

4. Join 4 of Unit 2 to form a full compass.

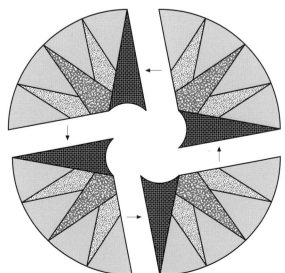

5. Appliqué a center circle to the compass.

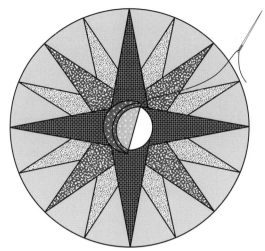

6. Appliqué the compass to the background square.

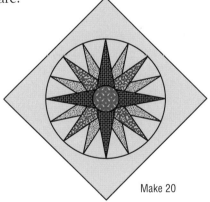

Make 20

Quilt Patch Pointer: Brenda likes to reverse-appliqué the background square to the compass. She feels it is easier to match the compass points to the circle, without the bulk of folding over the seam allowances. To do it Bren's way:

1. Use a compass to draft a circle on the background square with a radius that is ½ the finished diameter of your Mariner's Compass, not including seam allowances.
2. With sharp scissors, cut away the inside of the circle ¼" inside the pencil line.

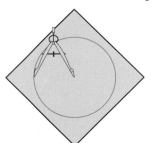 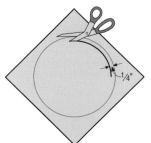

3. Carefully clip the circle, cutting almost to the pencil line. Space clips ¼" or more apart. Lay the background over the pieced compass and appliqué it to the compass, turning under the clipped edge.

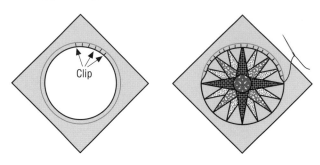

Assembling the Quilt

1. Arrange the Mariner's Compass blocks, alternating blocks, and side setting triangles as shown. Sew them together into diagonal rows. Press the seam allowances of the even-numbered rows in one direction and the seam allowances of the odd-numbered rows in the opposite direction.
2. Sew the rows together, matching the seams carefully. Add the corner triangles last.

Assembling and Adding the Borders

1. Sew together the inner border strips end to end. Measure across the width and length of the quilt. Trim the strips to fit and sew to the quilt top, referring to "Plain Borders" on page 16.
2. Sew together the 14 half-compass blocks as shown.

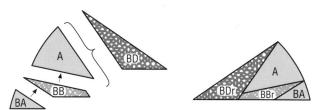

Make 2 for each block.

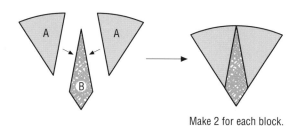

Make 1 for each half-compass.   Make 1 for each half-compass.

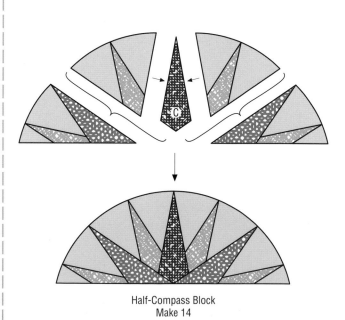

Half-Compass Block
Make 14

3. Sew together 4 corner half-compasses using pieces A, B, C, D, CD, and CDr. (Note: These are not the same as the other half-compasses. Keep them separate.)

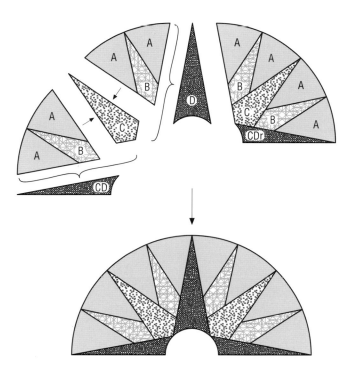

4. Sew together 4 quarter-compasses using pieces A, B, C, CD, and CDr.

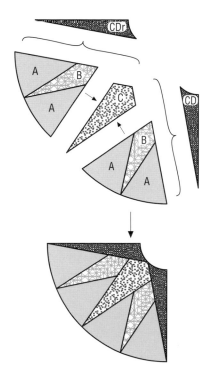

5. On the curve of the half-compass, corner half-compass, and quarter-compass units, fold the $1/4$"-wide seam allowance to the back and baste.

6. Measure the width of the quilt across the middle, and piece and trim 2 outer border strips to fit. Measure the length of the quilt across the middle. Add $10^{1}/_{2}$" to the length; piece and trim 2 border strips to that measurement.

7. Place the top and bottom border strips next to the quilt top. In the seam allowances of the outer borders, mark the points where the compass triangles in the quilt top touch the inner border.

8. Appliqué 3 half-compasses to each of the top and bottom border strips. Center them between the marks in the border seam allowance. Appliqué a quarter-compass to each end of the top and bottom border strips.

9. Sew the appliquéd border strips to the top and bottom of the quilt top.

10. Measure the quilt top. Trim border strips to fit if necessary. In the seam allowances of the side borders, mark the points where the compass blocks touch the inner border, the seams of the top and bottom borders, and the edges of the quarter-compass units.

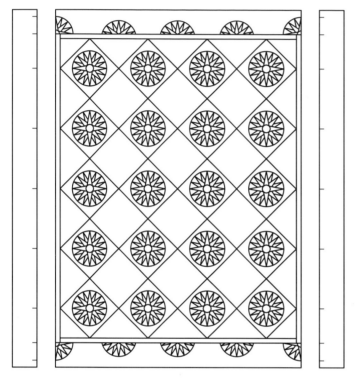

11. Appliqué 4 half-compasses to each of the side border strips, centering them between the marks in the seam allowances. Appliqué the corner half-compasses to the ends of the border strips, with their centers at the top and bottom border seam marks.

Corner
Half-Compass

Corner
Half-Compass

12. Sew the side borders to the sides of the quilt, carefully matching compass points in the corners.
13. Appliqué the center circles to the corner compasses. See step 5, page 63.

Finishing

1. Layer the quilt top with batting and backing. Baste the layers together.
2. Quilt as desired, or use the quilting designs provided on the pullout pattern.
3. Bind the edges of the quilt.
4. Label your quilt, step back, and smell the roses!

Elephants That March to a Different Drummer

By Judy A. House, 1993, Alexandria, Virginia, 27" x 42".

The name of this quilt represents very clearly the open mind and attitude Judy brings to the evolution of her unusual quilts. When Judy teaches her innovative design classes, every quilt comes out differently as her students work to achieve extensions of their personalities through quiltmaking. They march to their own beat throughout the design process.

If you are a free spirit, follow Plan A. If you require more direction, please keep reading for Plan B.

PLAN A

This is your quilt for you to design and enjoy. It's easy.

1. Select one or two focus fabrics.
2. Gather some solids and prints: lights, mediums, and darks that complement your focus fabrics.
3. Sew up a bunch of stars in many shapes and sizes. See pages 68–70.
4. Lay the stars out in a pleasing arrangement. Because they are different sizes, they will not fit together, leaving areas that Judy calls "blanks."
5. Cut squares, rectangles, and strips to fill in the blanks so that you can sew the quilt top together. See page 71.
6. Add borders and fuse or appliqué smaller stars in place.
7. Add batting, backing, and quilt away.

PLAN B
Materials: 44"-wide fabric

1½ yds. total of focus fabrics (1yd. would probably do, but you'd worry too much about running out.)
¾ yd. total of accent fabrics for stars (Judy used 12 different accent fabrics. Small pieces are sufficient.)
¼ yd. for inner border
⅜ yd. for outer border
½ yd. paper-backed fusible web
32" x 46" piece of batting

Judy prefers not to buy border fabric in advance, since she usually doesn't know which colors from the body of the quilt she'll want to emphasize. You can "interview" several different border fabrics, then purchase the exact amounts you need once the body of your quilt is complete.

Star #1 Variations

Make 1 each of the blocks shown below, cutting the pieces for each as listed in the cutting chart at right. Piece each star as directed in "Constructing Star #1", beginning on page 69.

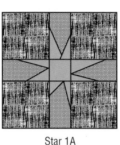
Star 1A

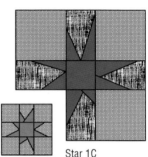
Star 1C

Star 1B

Star 1F

Star 1E

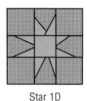
Star 1D

Star 1I

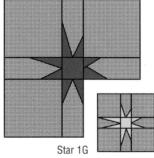
Star 1G

Star 1H

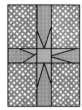
Star 1J

Cutting

Fabric		No. of Pieces	Dimensions
Star 1A	Focus	4	2" x 3³/₄"
		4	3³/₄" x 3³/₄"
	Accent	1	2" x 2"
		8	1³/₄" x 3"
Star 1B	Focus	4	1¹/₂" x 1³/₄"
		4	1³/₄" x 1³/₄"
	Accent	1	1¹/₂" x 1¹/₂"
		8	1" x 1¹/₂"
Star 1C	Focus	4	2¹/₂" x 4"
		3	4" x 4"
	Accent	1	2¹/₂" x 2¹/₂"
		8	1³/₄" x 3"
Star 1D	Focus	4	2" x 2³/₈"
		4	2³/₈" x 2³/₈"
	Accent	1	2" x 2"
		8	1¹/₄" x 1³/₄"
Star 1E	Focus	4	2¹/₄" x 5¹/₄"
		3	5¹/₄" x 5¹/₄"
	Accent	1	2¹/₄" x 2¹/₄"
		8	1³/₄" x 4"
Star 1F	Focus	4	1¹/₂" x 2³/₈"
		4	2³/₈" x 2³/₈"
	Accent	1	1¹/₂" x 1¹/₂"
		8	1¹/₂" x 2¹/₄"
Star 1G	Focus	4	2" x 4¹/₂"
		3	4¹/₂" x 4¹/₂"
	Accent	1	2" x 2"
		8	1¹/₂" x 3¹/₂"
Star 1H	Focus	4	1¹/₄" x 2¹/₈"
		4	2¹/₈" x 2¹/₈"
	Accent	1	1¹/₄" x 1¹/₄"
		8	1" x 2"
Star 1I	Focus	4	2¹/₄" x 2⁵/₈"
		4	2³/₈" x 2³/₈"
	Accent	1	2¹/₄" x 2¹/₄"
		8	1¹/₂" x 2¹/₂"
Star 1J	Focus	2	1¹/₂" x 3¹/₂"
		2	1¹/₂" x 2¹/₂"
		4	2¹/₂" x 3¹/₂"
	Accent	1	1¹/₂" x 1¹/₂"
		8	1¹/₄" x 2¹/₂"

Constructing Star #1

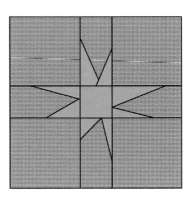

Star #1

To cut star pieces, refer to the cutting chart at left for required sizes. Cut the following pieces for each Star block.

1. Background: From one of your focus fabrics, cut 4 strips of the required length and width. Cut 4 corner squares that measure the same as the length of the strips.

2. Star: From an accent fabric, cut a square the same width as the focus-fabric strips. Cut 8 matching strips for star points.

Focus fabric   Focus fabric   Accent fabric   Accent fabric
Cut 4   Cut 4   Cut 1   Cut 8

3. Place an accent strip across one focus-fabric strip as shown. Sew a seam ¹/₄" from the edge of the accent strip. Open the accent fabric, press, and trim even with the edges of the focus strip.

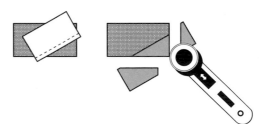

4. Using the same technique, sew the second star point to the strip. Make three more star-point units with the other focus-fabric and accent strips, changing the angle of the seam line for each star point.

Make 4

5. Arrange the center square, the star points, and the corner squares in rows. Sew the rows together, pressing the seams in Rows 1 and 3 outward and the seams in Row 2 toward the center.

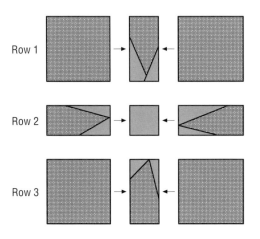

Row 1

Row 2

Row 3

6. Sew the rows together, matching the seams carefully.

Quilt Patch Pointer: You can vary the sizes and shapes of the Star blocks by changing the lengths and widths of the focus and accent strips. Judy suggests experimenting with rectangular centers for the stars.

Constructing Star #2

1. Using Star #2 block on page 73, make templates from plastic. See "Making Templates" on pages 9–10.
2. From the focus fabrics, cut 2 each of templates 1, 3, 4, 7, and 9. From the accent fabric, cut 2 each of templates 2, 5, 6, and 8. Mark the seam intersections on each piece for accurate piecing.
3. Sew the pieces together following the piecing diagram. Make 2 Star #2 blocks.

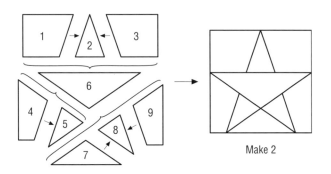

Make 2

Cutting Spacing Strips and Borders

Cut the following strips from the focus fabrics:

1 strip, 1½" x 9½", for piece a
1 strip, 1½" x 8½", for piece b
1 strip, 1½" x 18½", for piece c
1 strip, 4½" x 13", for piece d
1 strip, 4½" x 6", for piece e
1 strip, 3½" x 14½", for piece f
2 strips, each 1¾" x 4¾", for pieces g and h
1 strip, 2" x 5¾", for piece i
2 strips, each 3¾" x 4½", for pieces j and k
1 strip, 4½" x 6", for piece l
1 strip, 2¾" x 4¾", for piece m
1 strip, 2¼" x 7", for piece n
1 strip, 3¾" x 5½", for piece o
4 strips, 1¾" x 42", for inner borders
4 strips, 2¼" x 42", for outer borders

Assembling the Quilt

Referring to the quilt plan on page 72 and the illustrations below, arrange the Star blocks and the spacing strips. Sew them together in sections, then sew the sections together to complete the quilt top.

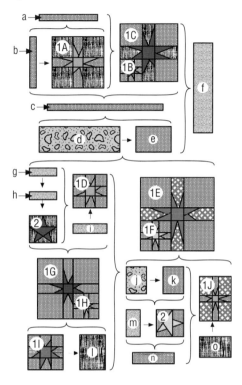

Simply fuse the remaining stars to the surface of the quilt. Trace the patterns on page 73 or draw your own onto paper-backed fusible web. Cut around the star and fuse it to the wrong side of one of your star fabrics. Cut out the star, place it on the surface of the quilt, and fuse in place. Finish the star edges with a satin stitch, buttonhole stitch, decorative overstitching, or free-motion machine quilting. Make at least 15 fusible stars, all different sizes, shapes, colors, and values, and "sprinkle" them across your quilt.

> ▶ **Quilt Patch Pointer:** The elephants on this quilt are part of the design of one of Judy's focus fabrics. You can use any design element you like in any spacing strip on your quilt, but if the elephants particularly please you, trace the pattern on page 73 and fuse some to your quilt.

Borders

1. Referring to "Plain Borders" on page 16, measure the quilt top. Trim and add the inner border strips, first to the sides, then to the top and bottom.
2. Measure the quilt with the inner borders and trim the outer border strips to these measurements.
3. Cut 4 corner squares, each 2" x 2". Cut 16 strips, each 1½" x 10", for corner star points. Following the method for construction of Star #1, add star points to the ends of the border strips.
   Add corner squares to the side border strips. Add the borders first to the top and bottom, then to the sides.

Top and Bottom Borders
Make 2

Side Borders
Make 2

Finishing

1. Layer the quilt top with batting and backing. Baste the layers together.
2. Quilt as desired.
3. Label your quilt.
   Judy hopes you had fun.

Star #2

1

2

3

4

5

6

7

8

9

Escaping the Herd

By Carolyn Lynch and The Dirty Dozen,
1992, Annandale, Virginia, 56¹/₂" x 69".

Every month the members of Carolyn's quilting group, The Dirty Dozen, make blocks for the meeting hostess. When it was Carolyn's turn, she requested blocks with the theme "I Never Saw a Purple Cow." Everyone received a piece of tan background fabric with the instruction to make any block that fit the theme, was washable, had right-angle corners, and did not exceed 12" x 16" in size. The setting, quilting, and other finishing details were done by Carolyn.

Carolyn changed the title to "Escaping the Herd," after the name of the block with the purple cow stepping out. It seemed an appropriate reflection of this somewhat irreverent and fun-loving group of quilters. The poem that inspired the theme, "I Never Saw a Purple Cow," is about conformity, something no one in the group espoused. Credit for each individual block design is given with the block instructions.

Materials: 44"-wide fabric

For blocks:

Choose scraps in a wide variety of colors and prints. You need:

tan, one piece at least 10" square for "She's Outstanding In Her Field"

day- and night-sky fabrics

pinks for udders and ears

purple lamé for sunglasses on Moo Town cow

several purple prints

white solids or prints

several black prints

one red print

greens for corn and crayon box

landscape fabrics

"cow" colors for crayons

several black and white "cow" prints

For backgrounds, sashing, borders, and binding:

1/4 yd. total of accent colors (purple print and "cow" print or check)

1 1/3 yds. total of black prints for sashing

2/3 yd. gray stripe for sashing

1 2/3 yds. gray print for border

2 yds. background fabric ("muddy" muslin) for blocks

3" x 12" scrap of purple print for triangles

1/2 yd. purple stripe for binding

4 yds. for backing

60" x 73" piece of batting

Embellishments

Embroidery floss in yellow, green, brown, black, and purple

7 miniature cowbells

12" of 1/8"-wide red ribbon

Black permanent-ink fabric marking pen

Cutting

Using the templates on the pullout pattern at the back of the book, cut pieces for each block. (See "Making Templates" on pages 9–10.) Make the blocks, following the directions on pages 76–83. See "Experimenting with Appliqué" on pages 13–15.

Cut the strips for sashing and borders as indicated below.

From accent fabrics, cut:

1 strip, 2 7/8" x 12". Crosscut into 4 squares, each 2 7/8" x 2 7/8", and cut each square once diagonally into a total of 8 triangles.

1 strip, 2 1/2" x 36. Crosscut into the following lengths:

2 1/2" x 6 1/2", for pieces LL and PP

2 1/2" x 21", for piece G

From black cow print or check, cut:

1 strip, 2 1/2" x 28". Crosscut into the following lengths:

2 1/2" x 12 7/8", for piece FF

2 1/2" x 14 7/8", for piece F

2 1/2" x 14 7/8", for piece CC

From black fabric, cut strips in the following lengths:

2 1/2" x 10 7/8", for piece K

2 1/2" x 12 7/8", for pieces E, Y, and BB

2 1/2" x 13 7/8", for piece W

2 1/2" x 14 7/8", for pieces C, B, M, and Q

2 1/2" x 16 7/8", for piece S

2 1/2" x 17 7/8", for piece U

2 1/2" x 18 7/8", for piece I

2 1/2" x 44 7/8", for piece GG

2 1/2" x 45 1/4", for piece N

From gray stripe, cut:

1 strip, 2 1/2" x 6 1/2", for piece II

3 strips, each 2 1/2" x 10 7/8", for pieces H, J, and L

2 strips, each 2 1/2" x 11 7/8", for pieces P and R

2 strips, each 2 1/2" x 12 7/8", for pieces D and EE

5 strips, each 2 1/2" x 13 7/8", for pieces O, X, Z, T, and V

1 strip, 2 1/2" x 14 7/8", for piece A

1 strip, 2 1/2" x 17 7/8", for piece AA

1 strip, 2 1/2" x 20 1/4", for piece DD

From gray print, cut:

1 strip, 6 1/2" x 12 1/2", for piece KK

1 strip, 6 1/2" x 14 1/2", for piece JJ

1 strip, 6 1/2" x 25 1/2", for piece QQ

1 strip, 6 1/2" x 29 1/2", for piece OO

1 strip, 6 1/2" x 42 1/2", for piece HH

1 strip, 6 1/2" x 44 1/2", for piece MM

1 strip, 6 1/2" x 56 1/2", for piece NN

She's Outstanding in Her Field

By Carol Duesi, Springfield, Virginia
Finished Size: 12" x 12"

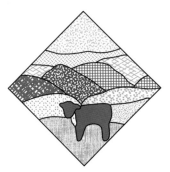

She's Outstanding in Her Field

1. Using the method of your choice, make templates for each of the block pieces on the pullout pattern. Cut pieces from scraps of fabric.
2. From background fabric, cut a square 7½" x 7½". Appliqué the pieces to the background in numerical order.
3. From tan fabric, cut two 5⅝" x 5⅝" squares. Cut each in half diagonally to yield a total of 4 triangles.
4. Sew the 4 large tan triangles to the Cow block.
5. Referring to "Making Half-Square Triangle Units" on pages 39–40, cut 2"-wide bias strips from 10" squares of the tan and background fabrics. Use template A on the pullout pattern to cut 36 half-square triangle units.

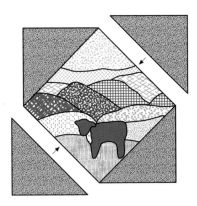

6. Referring to the color photo on page 74 for color placement, assemble 2 strips, using 8

half-square triangle units for each. Sew one to each side of the block.

Make 2 strips of 10 half-square triangle units, beginning and ending with a unit turned so that the dark triangle faces away from the block as shown. Sew the strips to the top and bottom edges of the block.

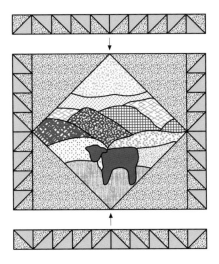

Fiberfill

By Dorothy Martin, Annandale, Virginia
Finished Size: 8" x 16"

Dorothy is a bonsai enthusiast and cares for several exceptional and expensive plants. The cow, of course, has chosen to nibble on one of her priceless treasures!

Fiberfill

1. From the background fabric, cut an 8½" x 16½" rectangle.

2. Using the design on the pullout pattern, make a template for each cow piece. Use template plastic or try the freezer-paper method in "I Never Saw A Purple Cow" on page 80. Cut out the pieces from scraps of fabric. Piece the cow body together as shown.

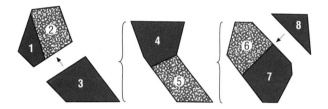

3. Sew the tail pieces together and add the tail to the body.

4. Make the leg/foot sections, sewing an udder to one set, and add them to the body.

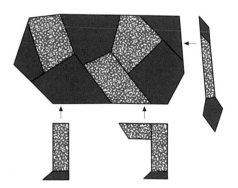

5. Cut 4 ears. Place 2 pieces right sides together and stitch as shown. Make 2 ears and sew them to the sides of the cow's head. Sew horns to the corners of the cow's head.

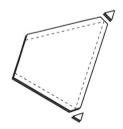

Sew ear pieces together.
Trim corners and turn right side out.

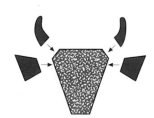

6. Appliqué the head and horns to the body as shown in the block diagram. Appliqué the cow to the background, leaving the ears loose.

7. Using black floss, embroider the eyes.

8. Bossy is nibbling on Dottie's prize bonsai tree. Use lazy daisy stitches to embroider the leaves falling from her mouth.

9. Appliqué the bowl and trunk of the bonsai tree to the background. Use green floss to embroider its foliage with clusters of lazy daisy stitches. See page 79.

10. Use brown floss to outline-stitch the dirt under the cow's feet and the bonsai bowl.

Bessie Steps Out

By Brenda Clements Jones, Arlington, Virginia
Finished Size: 8" x 8"

Bessie Steps Out

1. From night-sky fabric, cut an 8¹/₂" x 8¹/₂" square.

2. Using the appliqué technique of your choice, make templates from the design on the pullout pattern. Cut out pieces for the cow and moon from scraps of fabric. Appliqué the moon to the background.

3. String a miniature bell on the ¹/₈"-wide red ribbon and sew the ends to the sides of the cow's neck.

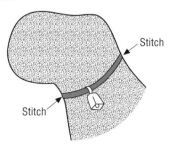

4. Make a tail using 3 strands of 6-ply embroidery floss. Slip it under her before appliquéing her to the background.
5. Appliqué the Bessie pieces to the block in numerical order.
6. Embroider Bessie's nose with pink floss, her eyelashes with black floss, and her heart-shaped mouth with red floss.

Moo Town

By Margaret Marks, Lee-on-the-Solent, Hampshire, England
Finished Size: 8" x 12"

Moo Town

1. From the background fabric, cut one 3¼" x 12½" strip.
2. Using the block design on the pullout pattern, prepare templates. Cut 1 each of templates 1–6 from the background fabric.
3. Cut 1 each of templates 7–11 from scraps of black-and-white fabrics.
4. Cut 1 template 12 from a wild purple print.
5. Arrange and sew the pieces into rows as shown. Press the seams in opposite directions from row to row. Sew the rows together to form the block.

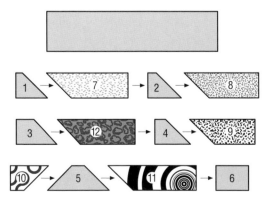

6. Make appliqué templates and cut out pieces for the udder, leg, spots, cow faces, and sunglasses. Using the block pattern as a placement guide, appliqué the pieces to the cow bodies.
7. Embroider eyes and mouths, or draw them with a permanent-ink fabric marking pen. (Keep in mind that they are "eyeing" the purple cow with suspicion, but she's cool.)

Dawlin' Clementine

By Sue White, Moyack, North Carolina
Finished Size: 10" x 10"

Dawlin' Clementine

1. From the background fabric, cut a 10½" x 10½" square.
2. Using the block design on the pullout pattern, prepare templates for pieces 1–15. From scraps of purple, white, and black fabrics, cut 1 of each.
3. Appliqué the Clementine pieces to the background in numerical order.
4. Using black floss, embroider the eyelashes with turkey work and the eyes with satin stitches.

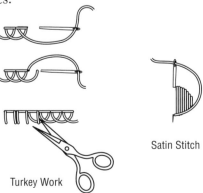

Turkey Work

Satin Stitch

I Never Saw . . .

By Paul Dick, Woodbridge, Virginia
Finished Size: 9" x 12"

I Never Saw . . .

1. From the background fabric, cut a
   9½" x 12½" rectangle.
2. Using the block design on the pullout pattern,
   prepare templates and cut 1 each of templates
   1–6 from white, purple, and the red print.
3. Appliqué the cow pieces to the background in
   numerical order.
4. Outline-stitch the
   leg and mouth
   with black floss.
   Satin-stitch the
   eyes (which are
   crossed, so she
   can't see) and
   embroider a cluster
   of French knots at
   the top of the head
   for "hair." Use tiny
   black buttons for
   the nostrils or satin
   stitch with black
   floss.

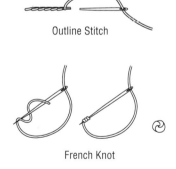

Outline Stitch

French Knot

Detached Chain or
Lazy Daisy Stitch

5. Embroider the
   daisies with yellow
   floss. Use green
   floss for the stems
   and grass.
6. Using outline stitches, embroider the saw in
   the upper right corner. Appliqué a red inter-
   national "NO!" symbol over the saw.
7. Embroider or write "I Never Saw . ." under
   the red circle.

Cowhide Colors of the World— A New Crayon Concept

By Laroletta Petty, Evergreen, Colorado
Finished Size: 9" x 14"

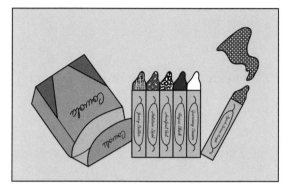

Cowhide Colors of the World—
A New Crayon Concept

1. From the background fabric, cut a 9½" x 14½"
   rectangle.
2. Using the cowola designs on the pullout
   pattern, make templates for the crayons, box,
   and "squiggle." Cut 1 of each template from
   the scraps of tan, green, cow colors, and a
   purple print.
3. Appliqué the pieces of the cowola box to the
   background in numerical order.
4. Appliqué the cowola tips and stem(s) in
   numerical order. (Machine stitch or quilt the
   lines that divide the cowolas.)
5. Appliqué the last tip and cowola and the
   purple "squiggle" to the background.
6. Using embroidery floss or a permanent-ink
   fabric marking pen, add the lettering to the
   cowolas, box, and background.

I Never Saw a Purple Cow

By Sandy Miller, Annandale, Virginia.
Original block by Margaret Rolfe from her book *Patchwork Quilts to Make for Children;* used with her permission.
Finished Size: 10" x 11"

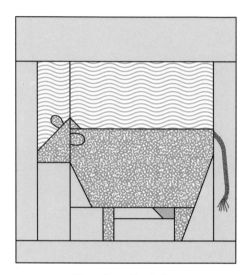

I Never Saw a Purple Cow

1. Using the block design on the pullout pattern, trace the entire block onto freezer paper and number the pieces as shown on the pattern. Cut apart the freezer-paper pieces and iron them to the *right* side of the appropriate fabric. Adding ¼" on all sides, cut out the pieces with a rotary cutter. Leave the paper in place until the block is completed.
2. Make a template for piece 1a and cut 1 from a scrap of purple print for the cow's right ear. Appliqué it to piece 1.

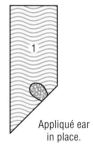

Appliqué ear
in place.

3. Make a template for piece 4a and cut 2 from a purple print for the cow's left ear. Pin them right sides together and machine stitch on the

stitching lines. Trim the seams, clip the curves, turn right side out, and press. Pin in place as shown for a 3-D ear.

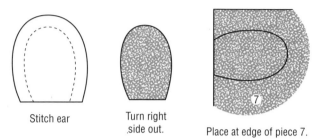

Stitch ear

Turn right
side out.

Place at edge of piece 7.

4. Sew together the cow pieces as shown.

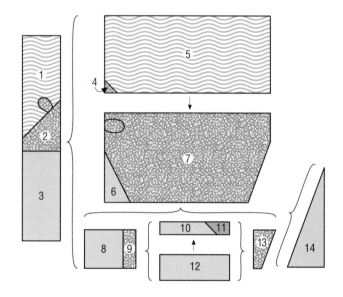

5. Make a tail, using three strands of 6-ply embroidery floss. Make a knot near the end and comb or unravel the end to make a tassel. Stitch in place.

6. From background fabric, cut 2 strips, each 1½" x 8½". Sew them to the sides of the block. Cut 1 strip, 1½" x 10½". Sew to the bottom edge of the block. Cut 1 strip, 2½" x 10½". Sew to top edge of the block.

High Heels Make Your Calves Look Sexy

By Betty Jo Blagdon, St. Inigoes, Maryland. Pattern by Betty Jo's husband, Alex Kampf. Finished Size: 11" x 15"

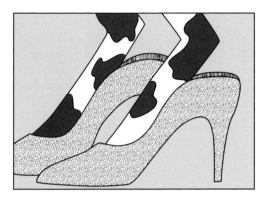

High Heels Make Your Calves Look Sexy

1. From background fabric, cut one 11½" x 15½" rectangle.
2. Prepare appliqué templates for pieces 1–11, using the block design on the pullout pattern. From scraps of purple, black, and white prints, cut 1 each of templates 1–11. Betty Jo suggests shoe fabric reminiscent of dyed-to-match satin prom shoes. Remember those?
3. Appliqué the high heels and cow "calves" to the background in numerical order.

High on Grass

By Carol Rutherford, Annandale, Virginia
Finished Size: 11" x 11"

High on Grass

1. From background fabric, cut an 11½" x 11½" square. From landscape fabrics, cut the field and grass.
2. From scraps of purples and pink prints, cut 1 each of templates 1–6, using the block pattern on the pullout.
3. Appliqué the field to the background, and the grass to the field.

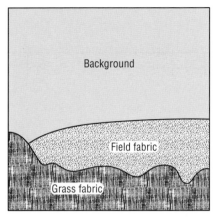

4. Cut 2 purple ear pieces and 2 pink ear pieces. Sew a purple to a pink ear piece, right sides together. Turn right side out and press. Fold the purple side halfway down over the pink side. Make 2 ears (a left and a right).

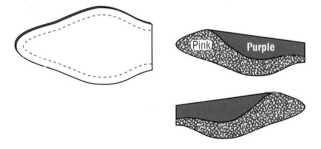

5. Cut a ³/₄" x 4" strip of purple print. Fold in half, right sides together. Place a few strands of floss inside and stitch ¼" from the long edge. Turn right side out and press. Fringe should now be hanging from the end of the tail.

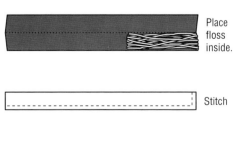

Place floss inside.

Stitch

Turn right side out.

6. Place some floss fringe between the cow's ears for bangs. Stitch across the floss, close to the edge of the piece, to hold the bangs in place.

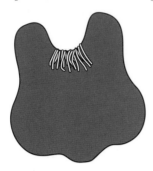

7. Appliqué all pieces to the background in numerical order.
8. Use gold floss to satin-stitch the eyes. Outline-stitch the eyelashes and mouth using black floss. Give her a happy expression. She's a contented cow.
9. Attach a bow made with a ⅛" x 12" piece of ribbon.

Cow Barn

By Mary Balserak, Fairfax, Virginia.
Adapted from an original block by Carolyn Lynch.
Finished Size: 10" x 10"

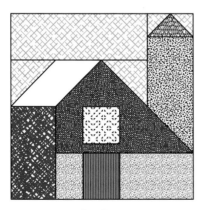

Cow Barn

1. Referring to the freezer-paper template method in "I Never Saw a Purple Cow" on page 80, make templates for each of the Cow Barn pieces on the pullout pattern. Cut out the pieces from scraps of fabric. (For the barn

window, choose a fabric with an appropriate design and place the upper barn template on the fabric to give the effect of a window that is open or closed.)
2. Sew the pieces together as shown.

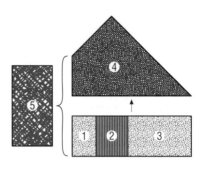

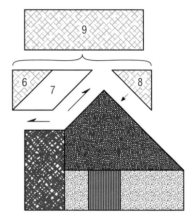

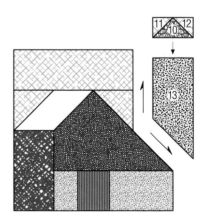

3. Appliqué the barn window to the upper barn front.

Escaping the Herd

By Pat Gallagher, Annandale, Virginia
Finished Size: 6" x 32"

Escaping the Herd

1. From background fabric, cut a 6¹/₂" x 32¹/₂" rectangle.
2. Make a cow template, using the design on the pullout pattern. Cut 5 cows from black-and-white prints. Appliqué them to the background.
3. Sew miniature bells at the necks of the cows.
4. From a purple print, cut 1 cow. This cow overlaps the sashing; appliqué her to the block after sewing the sashing to the blocks. Sew her bell to her tail. She wants to know if the grass is really greener . . .

Lend Me Your Ear

By Judy Babb, Fairfax, Virginia.
This is a variation of an original block from the pattern "Mr. MacGregor's Garden" by *Quilts & Other Comforts* and is used with their permission.
Finished Size: 10" x 15"

Lend Me Your Ear

1. From background fabric, cut a 10¹/₂" x 15¹/₂" rectangle.
2. Using the block design on the pullout pattern, make templates and cut 1 each of pieces 1–17 from scraps of green and yellow prints. Appliqué the pieces to the background in numerical order.
3. Embroider or use a permanent-ink fabric marker to write the words "Lend Me Your Ear" at the bottom of the block.

Adding Sashing and Borders

Sashing Preparation and Sewing
1. Trim one end at a 45° angle and sew a purple triangle to pieces C, F, N, O, Z, CC, DD, and FF as shown.

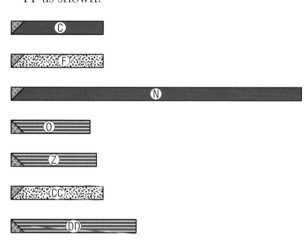

2. Sew the sashing strips around each block in alphabetical order, mitering the corners where indicated in the following steps. Start or stop stitching ¹/₄" from the corner of the block. To miter corners, follow the steps 4–6 on page 16.

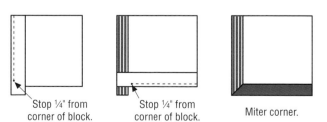

Stop ¼" from corner of block.   Stop ¼" from corner of block.   Miter corner.

Section Assembly and Borders

1. For the Dawlin' Clementine block, sew pieces D and E to the block and miter the corner. Sew piece F to the top of the block. Sew piece G to the right side. Begin stitching at the block/sashing seam line and stop about 3" from the bottom of the block. The seam will be finished when the Cow Barn is added later in the assembly process. Miter the upper corner.

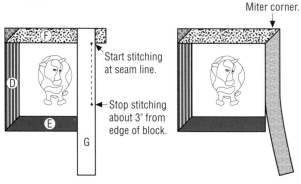

Miter corner.

Start stitching at seam line.

Stop stitching about 3" from edge of block.

2. Sew sashing strips A, B, and C to the "She's Outstanding in Her Field" block. Miter the corner between sashing strips A and B. Sew this block to the top of Dawlin' Clementine to make Section 1.

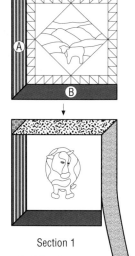

Section 1

3. Sew the sashing strips to each block in Section 2. Miter the corners. Sew the blocks together. Sew piece N to the top and, piece O to the right side; miter the corner.

4. Sew the sashing strips to each block in Section 3. Miter the corners. Sew the blocks together. When stitching the "Escaping the Herd" block to the bottom edge, start stitching at the right edge and stop about 5" from the left corner.

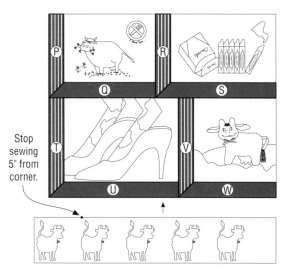

Stop sewing 5" from corner.

Section 3

5. Sew the sashing strips to each block in Section 4. Miter the corners between X and Y, AA and BB, and CC and DD. Sew the blocks together.

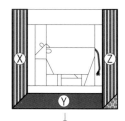

Section 4

Miter corner.

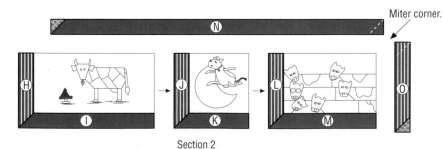

Section 2

6. Sew Section 3 to Section 4. Start stitching at the top and stop about 5" from the bottom.

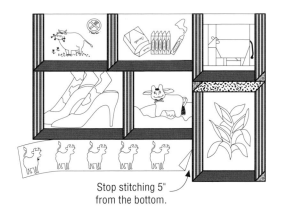

Stop stitching 5" from the bottom.

7. Sew Section 2 to the top edge of Section 3/4.

8. Sew Section 1 to Section 2/3/4. Sew the remaining portion of the Escaping the Herd block to the bottom of the Section 1 sashing strip.

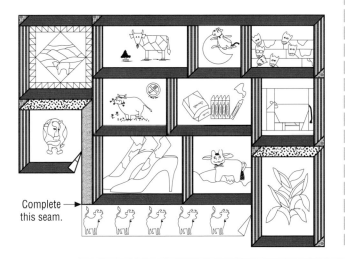

Complete this seam.

9. Sew pieces EE and FF to the Cow Barn block. Sew the block to the bottom of Section 1. Finish the remaining seam from Section 1 down the right side of the Cow Barn block.

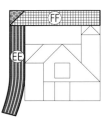

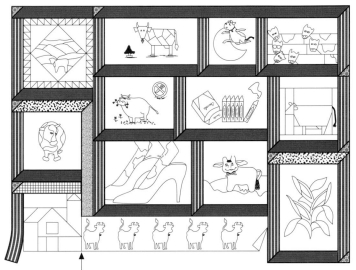

Finish remaining seam.

10. Sew piece GG below the Cow Barn and Escaping the Herd blocks. Refer to the illustration on page 86. Miter the left-hand corner. Finish the remaining seam between Sections 3 and 4. Appliqué the last cow on the Escaping the Herd block so that it overlaps onto the sashing strip.

Seated: Carol Duesi, Paul Dick, Judy Babb, Carolyn Lynch, Sandy Miller, Pat Gallagher, Brenda Jones, Dot Martin.

Standing: Sue White, Mary Balserak, Betty Jo Blagdon, Rosemary Tremba, Leslie Pfeifer.

Not Pictured: Laroletta Petty and Margaret Marks.

11. Assemble each of the pieced borders as shown below. Sew the top and bottom borders to the quilt top; then add the side borders.

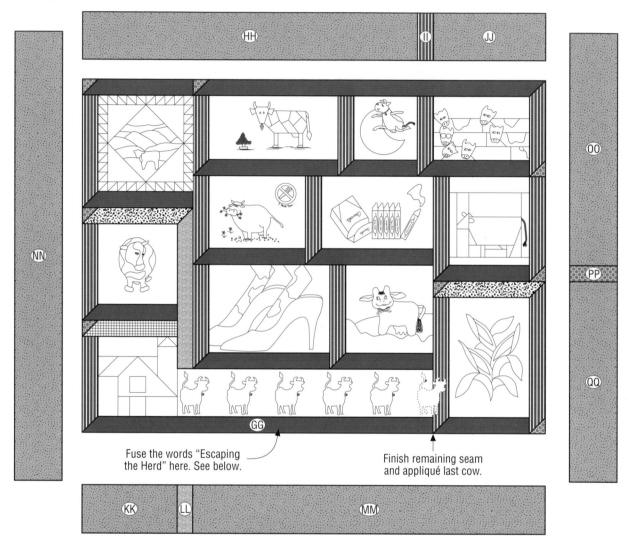

Fuse the words "Escaping the Herd" here. See below.

Finish remaining seam and appliqué last cow.

Finishing

1. Trace the words "Escaping the Herd" from the pullout pattern, or a title of your choosing, onto paper-backed fusible web. (Remember to trace the letters in reverse.) Referring to "Fusible Appliqué" on page 15, cut the letters apart, fuse them to a purple fabric, and then fuse the letters to the black sashing below the block, as shown above. If desired, use a fine-point permanent-ink pen to write the block names on the quilt top as indicated on the pullout pattern.

2. Using purple floss, buttonhole-stitch around the letters to secure the edges.
3. Layer the quilt with batting and backing. Baste the layers together.
4. Quilt the individual blocks with designs that enhance each block. Quilt a diagonal grid in the backgrounds if desired.
5. Quilt the border with the cowbell and rope designs on the pullout pattern.
6. Bind the edges of the quilt.

Carolyn and the Dirty Dozen hope you have a great time with this quilt. If you come up with any original blocks of your own on this theme we'd all love to see them, so send us a photo.

Connected Salzburgs

By Jennifer Heffernan, 1992, Falls Church, Virginia, 69" x 88".

This quilt is based on the block "Salzburg Connection" by Jinny Beyer from her book Patch-work Portfolio and is used with her permission. Jennifer never makes simple quilts. She looks for a pattern she likes and then experiments with its design possibilities. Most often a quilt develops as she makes it. She solves construction problems as they arise. As a result, Jennifer's quilts are unique both artistically and structurally. This quilt is hand pieced because there seemed no way to simplify it for machine-piecing without sacrificing design. It is not for the faint of heart or the beginning quilter.

Materials: 44"-wide fabric

1 yd. total of 2 dark prints for triangles (or 1½ to 2 yds. border stripe)

⅝ yd. medium print for piece 2

1½ yds. dark border stripe for pieces 4 and 4 reversed (dark blocks)

3½ yds. light background (1¾ yds. for blocks and 1½ yds. for the area between blocks and border)

1 yd. medium border stripe for pieces 4 and 4 reversed (light blocks)

1½ yds. accent for diamonds (1 yd. for vertical diamonds and ½ yd. for horizontal diamonds)

3 yds. border stripe for border

5¼ yds. for backing

¾ yd. for binding

73" x 95" piece of batting

Cutting

Use templates 1–8 on pages 91–92. To set in pieces more easily, mark seam intersections on the wrong side of fabric pieces.

From the dark prints or border stripe, cut:
200 template 1

From the medium print, cut:
200 template 2

From the dark border stripe, cut:
120 template 4
120 template 4 reversed

From the light background, cut:
200 template 3
200 template 3 reversed
18 template 6
18 template 6 reversed
4 template 7
4 template 7 reversed
8 template 8

From the medium border stripe, cut:
80 template 4
80 template 4 reversed

From the accent fabric cut:
169 template 5 (110 for vertical diamonds, 59 for horizontal diamonds)

From the border fabric, cut:
4 strips, 5½" x 92" (Customize the border width to accommodate the width of the print.)

Block Assembly

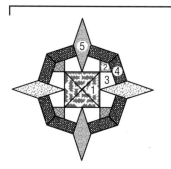

Block A
Make 15 dark blocks.
Make 12 medium blocks.

Block B
Make 15 dark blocks.
Make 8 medium blocks.

1. Sew together 4 triangles for the center square.

Make 50

2. Sew pieces 3 and 3r to piece 2.

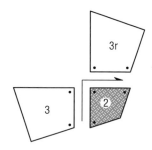

Sew a continuous seam in the direction shown.
Make 200

3. Add pieces 4 and 4r to the corner units from step 2, matching marked seam intersections.

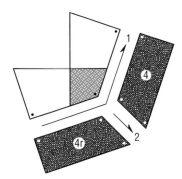

Make 120 dark.

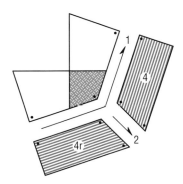

Make 80 medium.

4. Add a corner unit to each corner of the center square, matching marked seam intersections carefully.

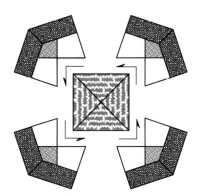

Sew in the direction of the arrows.
Make 30 dark.
Make 20 medium.

5. To complete Block A, sew 4 diamonds (piece 5) to the unit from step 4, matching marked seam intersections. (If you use two diamond colors, be sure to place the vertical diamond fabric and the horizontal diamond fabric as shown.)

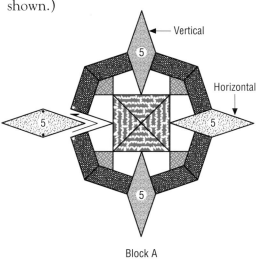

Block A
Make 12 medium.
Make 15 dark.

6. To complete Block B, add 2 diamonds (on opposite sides) to the unit from step 4. (If you use two diamond colors, use the vertical diamond fabric for all B blocks.)

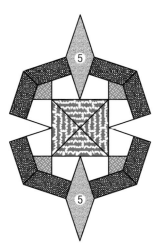

Block B
Make 8 medium.
Make 15 dark.

Assembling the Quilt

1. Arrange the blocks into horizontal rows, alternating A and B blocks. Use dark blocks for Rows 1, 3, 5, 7, and 9. Use medium blocks for Rows 2, 4, 6, and 8. (See illustration below.)

2. To join the blocks, set the diamond in each A block into the side opening of the adjacent B block. Stitch from the intersection of pieces 3 and 3 reversed to the marked side points of the diamond. *If you use two diamond colors, be sure to align the blocks correctly.*

3. Sew the rows together, setting in the diamonds of each row between the blocks of the row above.

4. Add diamonds between the blocks of the top and bottom rows. Refer to quilt plan at right.

5. Sew pieces 6, 6r, 7, and 7r to the top of Row 1 and to the bottom of Row 9. Sew pieces 6 and 6r to the ends of the even-numbered rows. Refer to the quilt plan at right.

Rows 1, 3, 5, 7, 9

Rows 2, 4, 6, 8

6. Add piece 8 to fill in spaces around the outside edge of the quilt top and "square off" the quilt.

7. Referring to "Borders with Mitered Corners" on page 16, measure the quilt top, add border strips, and miter the corners.

Finishing

1. Layer the quilt with batting and backing. Baste the layers together.
2. Quilt as desired.
3. Bind the edges of the quilt.
4. Label your quilt.

Congratulations! Enjoy your masterpiece!

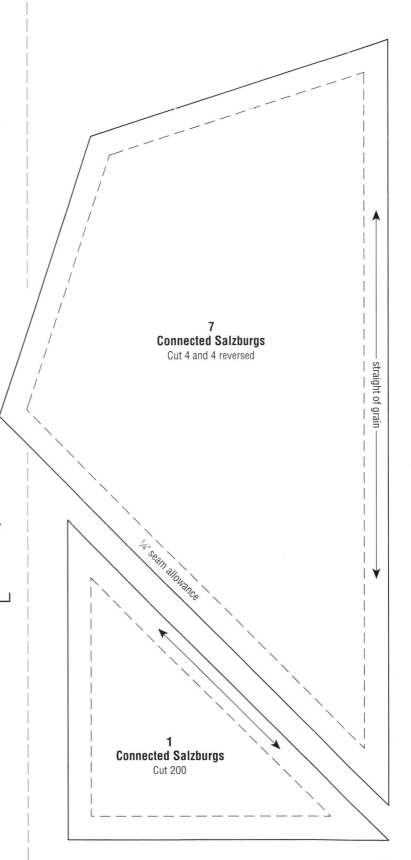

7
Connected Salzburgs
Cut 4 and 4 reversed

straight of grain

¼" seam allowance

1
Connected Salzburgs
Cut 200

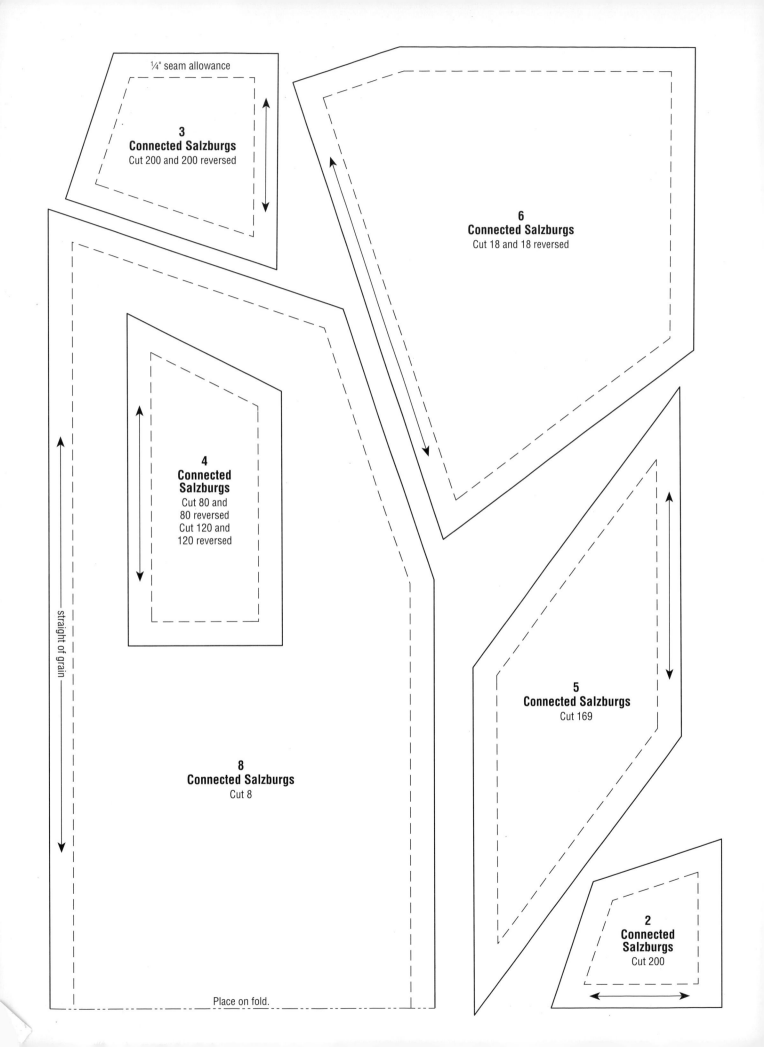

¼" seam allowance

3
Connected Salzburgs
Cut 200 and 200 reversed

6
Connected Salzburgs
Cut 18 and 18 reversed

4
Connected Salzburgs
Cut 80 and 80 reversed
Cut 120 and 120 reversed

straight of grain

5
Connected Salzburgs
Cut 169

8
Connected Salzburgs
Cut 8

2
Connected Salzburgs
Cut 200

Place on fold.